THE GROWING FAMILY SERIES

Growing Together

A Parent's Guide to Baby's First Year

Growing Together

A Parent's Guide to Baby's First Year

William Sears, M.D.

La Leche League International
Franklin Park, Illinois

July 1987
© 1987 by William Sears, M.D.
All rights reserved
First printing, July 1987
Second printing, July 1993

Printed in the United States of America
Photos by William and Martha Sears
Illustrations by Debbie Maze
Book and cover design by Kim Stuffelbeam
Edited by Gwen Gotsch
Library of Congress Card Catalog Number 87-81825
ISBN 0-912500-36-0

Dedicated to my son Matthew
and our first year of growing together.

Contents

This book arose out of an experiment in parenting. Matthew was our sixth baby and possibly our last. To capture every subtle change during Matthew's first year, my wife, Martha, and I observed, recorded, and evaluated every major (and sometimes minor) development in Matthew's behavior: what he did when, why he did it, our responses to his cues, and his responses to ours. This is the biographical method of studying infant development, which I learned from the writings of the famous biologist, Jean Piaget.

Our observations of Matthew during the first year were aided by technological devices: tape recorder, video camera, and, as you will see throughout this book, still photography. But first and foremost, our observation and recording of Matthew's development was done with our eyes, ears, and hands. Coincident with the observations of Matthew, I serially recorded the development of over one hundred of my new patients during their first year. All of this data provided the material for this book.

As I developed my skills as a mother and baby watcher, I discovered that not only was I enjoying my son more, but Martha and I were also developing as parents. I had always understood what a parent does for the baby, but I never before realized what the baby does for the parents. Once we learned to listen and respond, Matthew brought out the best in us. Because we tried to figure out his feelings, we became more sensitive to him. Because we were attentive to his major accomplishments, we became more observant of his more subtle triumphs. Because we understood him more, we enjoyed him more. We knew Matthew, he knew us. He was growing, we were growing—we were growing together.

My three goals in writing this book—and in all the books of the Growing Family Series—is to help you know your baby, to help you and your baby feel right, and to help all of you to enjoy one another.

ACKNOWLEDG-MENTS

My thanks go to the following:

To Gwen Gotsch, for her untiring editing; to Judy Torgus, for reading the manuscript; and to the other members of La Leche League International's Publications Department;

To the many parents and babies in my medical practice who contributed observations and developmental material;

To Debbie Maze whose illustrations clarify some of the more abstract features of attachment parenting and cognitive development;

To Jim and Bob Sears who typed the manuscript;

And, finally, a very special thank-you to my wife, Martha, who provided much material, insight, and wisdom for this book.

William Sears
June 1987

CHAPTER ONE:

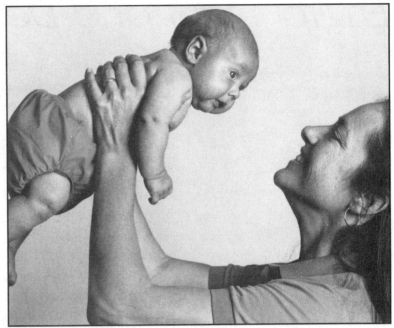

Maximizing Your Baby's Development

"What can we do to help our baby be a happier baby, a brighter baby?" "How can we assist our baby to develop to her fullest potential?" "What is my baby going to be able to do and when?" "How can I watch, with more understanding, as my baby grows? How can I encourage him each step along the way?"

Parents often ask these questions throughout their baby's first year. They want the best for their babies, and they also want to enjoy their role as parents. This book is designed to help you follow your baby's development through the first year. By understanding the many ways in which he is learning and growing, you will be able to know your baby better, encourage his development, and enjoy your time together.

Environment and Development

You can make a difference in your baby's development! During the last fifteen years, exciting new research has given parents and infant care professionals a deeper understanding of infant development. This new research has shown that an infant's environment greatly affects how he develops.

Until recently, experts thought of infant development as a sort of elevator. As the baby increased in age, he went up from one floor to the next. At each floor, the door opened automatically and some new skill got on. Given a reasonable amount of nurturing, health care, and adequate nutrition, baby would grow and attain the usual developmental milestones, more or less automatically, according to his or her own genetic and temperament characteristics.

While it is true that each baby's potential is genetically determined, how close the infant comes to reaching his potential is greatly affected by the responsiveness and the nurturing of his care-giving environment. In terms of the elevator analogy, the baby reaches each developmental floor already equipped with certain competencies. How these competencies develop into skills depends on the baby's interaction with the environment that he finds on each floor. This means that parenting style can enhance the development of a baby. Also, by observing and participating in the development of their baby, parents develop their own abilities, right along with their baby.

This book focuses not only on the development of the baby and the development of the parents, but also on the interaction between parents and infant, in other words, the development of a relationship. One tiny word describes that relationship: fit. By

Parenting style enhances development.

learning to fit together, parents and baby bring out the best in each other.

In the parenting profession there are lessons to be learned from history. In order for parents and infants to develop optimally, they must spend time with each other in meaningful interaction so that they can learn to fit together.

In the past, the great importance of interaction between parent and child has not always been recognized. The history of childcare and parenting in the twentieth century has been one of separation between mother and baby. Increasing use of technology in childbirth, the decline of breastfeeding, and various "scientific" approaches to child-rearing have all created obstacles to mother-infant attachment. Until the early 1970s "experts" had the upper hand, and parents followed the advice of authority figures rather than trusting their own intuition.

Then a profound change occurred. Parents began realizing the experts' system was not working, and they began changing their parenting style. They also asked for changes in the system. Consequently, today mothers and babies are able to remain together in the hospital after birth. Most mothers start out breastfeeding their babies and breastfeed longer. More parents are now sleeping with their babies and are carrying their babies in a variety of slings and carriers rather than leaving them in cribs, carriages, or strollers. Recent studies in infant development support what intuitive mothers have known all along: that parents and babies develop better if they have the opportunity to become securely attached to one other. It is as if science was giving mothers permission to follow their intuition. The term "bonding" has come into vogue, as if to put a modern scientific stamp of approval on the intuitive art of mothering. As Eleanor Randall of La Leche League International said, "I wonder if the term

HISTORICAL PERSPECTIVE

bonding gained such popularity because of the need to repair all that was damaged by unnecessary interference." Mothers have now been given permission to mother in a way that feels right to them. Fathers, so long portrayed as well-meaning but bumbling, have begun to take a more active part in infant care and have discovered that they have their own unique contributions to make to their infant's development.

The "superbaby" phenomenon represents a bit of overreaction to earlier ideas about infant development. It overemphasizes the role of parents as teachers rather than as playful companions and sensitive nurturers. An appropriate balance must be struck between stimulation, education, and nurturing.

I feel that the coming years will be looked upon as a golden age of parenting and a good time to be a baby. Both parents and babies will profit from an environment in which parents learn to recognize their infant's preferences and capabilities and also provide intuitive nurturing.

Developing a Parenting Style

During the first year, mother, father, and baby learn to come together as a family—to fit. This tiny word aptly describes the early relationship between baby and parents. Fitting together brings a sense of completeness to a relationship, a rightness that brings out the best in both parents and baby.

In the early weeks of parenting, well-meaning advisors will bombard you with advice on how to care for your baby. Everyone has a personal list of "how to's" for baby care. But it's your baby, not anyone else's. Learning how to care for your baby means developing an overall parenting style which allows the important "how to's" to follow naturally. Because of the wide variety of family circumstances, the variabilities of individual mothers, and the different needs of mothers, there are naturally a wide variety of parenting styles.

During my fifteen years of pediatric practice, I have observed all sorts of parenting styles, and my wife, Martha, and I have practiced various styles in parenting our own six children. The style of parenting which I advocate throughout this book is a style I call attachment parenting. It helps most growing families to develop a good fit. I feel that it is good for both parents and babies. Here's how you can make the style your own.

Attachment at birth. The days and weeks after birth are a sensitive period in which mothers and babies are uniquely primed to want to be close to each other. A close attachment after birth allows the natural, biological, attachment-promoting behaviors of the infant and the intuitive, biological, care-giving qualities of the mother to come together. Both members of this biological pair get off to the right start at a time when the infant is most needy and the mother is most ready to nurture.

Learn from your baby. Be open to the cues of your baby and respond according to your intuition. Try not to approach your parenting with a rigid set of rules such as, "I'm going to get my baby on a schedule" or "My baby will sleep through the night at six weeks." While you may be blessed with a baby who is an "easy" baby by temperament and who follows a schedule, you might be equally blessed with a high need baby who demands a more flexible parenting style.

Every baby comes wired with certain needs; if these needs are satisfied, the baby has a greater chance of developing to his full potential. Babies also come wired with attachment-promoting behaviors which

ATTACHMENT PARENTING

enable them to communicate their needs to their caregivers. For example, babies who need a lot of holding will protest if they are put down. Parents also come wired with intuitive abilities to respond and give. Part of developing a good fit during the first year is adjusting the response level of the parents to match the need level of the baby. Baby gives a cue, and mother and father, because they are open and tuned into the baby, respond to the cue. As the members of the family repeatedly rehearse this kind of communication, the baby learns to cue better and the parents learn to respond better. In time, parents and baby begin to flow together, developing a harmony between the cue and the appropriate response. They learn to fit.

Respond to cries. Give a nurturing response to your baby's cries. A baby's cry is designed for the survival of the baby and the development of the parents. Not responding to a cry disturbs the fit. By allowing yourself to offer a nurturing response to your baby's cry, instead of holding yourself back, you learn to respond better. In time, you learn to read baby's pre-cry signals and respond to those. This makes it possible for baby to learn other ways of communicating his needs. Your baby learns to cry "better," to make his needs known more effectively. Giving a nurturing response to baby's cries is one way parents can enhance baby's communicative skills. As one mother put it, "My baby never cries. She doesn't need to."

Beware of those ubiquitous advisors who unintentionally disturb the fit by suggesting that it is better to "let the baby cry it out" or who tell you that "he's just exercising his lungs." It is very easy for someone else to advise you to let your baby cry. Your advisor is not tuned in to your baby. He or she is outside the fit that you and your baby enjoy.

Breastfeed with infant-led weaning. There is a growing body of research which shows that breastfeeding enhances the growth, health, and development of the baby. Here are just a few of the advantages of breastfeeding your baby.

Human milk contains the amino acid taurine which promotes brain growth. Human milk also contains a special growth factor which stimulates DNA (the genetic building blocks within each cell), promoting cellular growth (Carpenter 1980). Breastfed newborns are more alert. Prolonged breastfeeding may enhance development. Dr. Ruth Lawrence, in her book, *Breastfeeding: A Guide for the Medical Profession*, states:

> Animal work has also shown the relationship of weaning time to learning skills. Since it has become evident that there are species-specific proteins and amino acids, it is possible that the brain develops more physiologically with the precise basic nutrients. Comparisons with animal species show that the more intelligent and skillful groups within the species are nursed longer.

In one study in Great Britain, breastfed babies started to walk two months earlier than bottle-fed babies (Douglas 1950). The longer the infant was nursed, the more striking the differences. In another study breastfed children scored higher on language and reading tests when in school. More prospective controlled studies are needed to substantiate these findings.

I know of no other biological interaction that contributes more to a good fit than nursing according to your baby's cues. I use the term nursing here because it suggests more than a method of feeding; it also implies a way of comforting. Nursing at the breast is a natural way of comforting a baby. Breastfeeding on cue encourages you to watch your baby for signs of hunger or stress rather than watching the clock or following some arbitrary outside schedule which interferes with the harmony you and your baby are developing. If all babies were meant to be fed on the same three- or four-hour schedule, they would also have the same temperament and

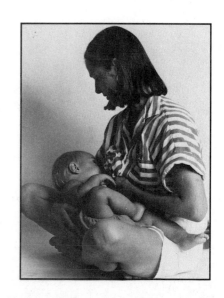

the same growth patterns, which they do not. Cue feeding helps you to learn to read your baby's needs. You have the satisfaction of watching a feeling of rightness overcome your baby as he molds against your breast when his distress is immediately followed by comfort. As your baby nurses, you both feel that in times of need this is where baby belongs and fits.

Don't limit your breastfeeding to a predetermined length of time. Follow your baby's cues. Life is a series of weanings— from the womb, from the breast, from home to school, from school to work. When a child is pushed into one of these steps before he is ready, he is at risk for less-than-ideal emotional development. Contact La Leche League if you need support for breastfeeding your child until he is ready to wean.

Wear your baby. One of the most exciting developments in parenting styles in the 1980s is that babies are now being "worn" in baby carriers rather than wheeled around in strollers or carriages. Holding your baby a lot, whether in a carrier or in your arms, may mean changing your attitude toward holding babies. You may feel that your baby is a separate person, but he may not know that yet. With most babies, especially those with intense needs, it helps to consider baby's gestation period as totalling eighteen months: nine months inside the womb and nine months outside. The baby needs to go on feeling a secure womb-like environment—the feeling he gets from being in your arms.

Some new parents feel that they should hold their babies just long enough to comfort them. Then they put them down again, as if periods of holding the baby are just brief interruptions in what the baby should be doing—lying in his crib or bassinette, soothing and entertaining himself. But research has shown that carrying babies actually benefits behavior and development. In one study, babies who were carried more showed enhanced visual alertness (Korner 1970). In another study, babies who were carried more in the early weeks cried 43 percent less later on (Hunziker 1986).

Wearing your baby in a carrier allows him to become accustomed to your body movements and to see things from your vantage point—both mother's and father's. The infant learns about life from being with humans. Baby's feeling of fitting in continues even when parents are on the go.

Share sleep with your baby. Be open to trying various sleeping arrangements. Babies usually give parents cues as to where they sleep the best. Some babies sleep best in their own rooms; others sleep best in a bed in their parents' room; many babies sleep best in their parents' bed. Wherever all three of you sleep the best is the right arrangement for you. Sharing sleep assures that baby will feel that he fits during the night as well as the day.

The arrangement of sharing sleep (baby, mother, and father in the same bed) is gradually becoming a more accepted style of parenting in the western world. Night feedings are easier when mother and baby are in close proximity to one another. Sleeping close to each other allows mother and baby to get their sleep cycles in synchrony. Both are likely to awaken at the same time to nurse and fall back to sleep easily. Baby does not have to cry nor mother leave her nest to fill nighttime needs. Newborns get their day-night sleep cycles organized more quickly when they share sleep with their mothers. This style of nighttime parenting is especially valuable for mothers who must be away from their babies during the day. Researchers have long recognized the value of touch for enhancing infant growth and development. Sharing sleep gives infants and parents lots of added touching.

Respond to your baby's language. In studying the effects of the environment on infant development researchers have found that the single most important factor which influenced a child's cognitive development was the responsiveness of the parent. The way parents interact with their infants, especially during infant-initiated play, contributes to a feeling of self-worth. When you pick up on, reinforce, and reciprocate your infant's cues, baby becomes more motivated to improve his skills. When a baby is given choices, he develops preferences. When a baby's cues are responded to, he develops trust. When a baby's competencies are reinforced, he develops more skills. Despite all the publicity about enriching an infant's surroundings, it is important to remember that it is the parents themselves, not the things they provide, who make a child's environment rich and responsive to his needs.

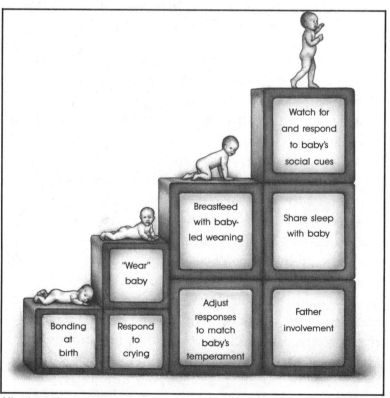

Attachment parenting

Father involvement. The above styles of parenting do not work as well without the father being actively involved in nurturing his infant. Fathers help to provide an environment which allows mothers to nurture their babies. Also, fathers are more than mother substitutes. They have their own unique contribution to make to the growth and development of their infants.

There are scientific reasons for believing that the attachment style of parenting optimizes the growth and development of infants and parents. The way infants are cared for profoundly affects their physical, emotional, social, and intellectual development.

Babies need lots of contact. Humans are a continuous contact species. One of my reasons for concluding that the attachment style of parenting is best for babies is based on the assumption that the nature of the milk produced by the female of each species indicates something about how the young should be cared for. In some animals, the mother is away from her young for many hours at a time. These mothers produce a milk very high in protein and fat so that feedings can be few and widely spaced. These animals are called intermittent contact species. Human milk, however, is relatively low in fat and protein, suggesting that the human infant needs frequent feedings and extensive maternal contact. Human infants and their mothers are a continuous contact species.

Separation from the mother may affect baby's body chemistry. Infants separated from their mothers have elevated levels of stress hormones, biological evidence of stress. However, babies who are not securely attached to a mother figure do not show this stress reaction. This suggests that the quality of the mother-infant relationship may affect the baby's hormonal system (Ainsworth, 1979). This also

HOW ATTACHMENT PARENTING AFFECTS DEVELOPMENT

accounts for the observation that the babies with the greatest attachment to their mothers are the ones who protest most vehemently when separated.

Attachment parenting also does something healthy for the mother. It promotes the secretion of the hormone prolactin. This hormone, which has been called "the mothering hormone," may provide a biological basis for mothers' intuition. Prolactin is secreted very rapidly into the mother's blood stream in response to the baby's sucking at the breast, but the levels fall off within an hour. Frequent breastfeeding (and thus, frequent contact between mother and baby) is necessary to keep the mother's baseline prolactin levels high.

Attachment parenting helps babies (and parents) thrive. All infants grow, but not all infants thrive. Thriving takes growth one step further and means growth to the fullest potential. Research has shown that the attachment style of parenting helps babies thrive. Infants thrive better with mothers who are sensitively responsive (Bowlby 1969; Ainsworth 1978). Infant animals who stay close to their mothers have higher levels of growth hormone and enzymes essential for brain growth. Separation from the mother or a lack of interaction with her when she was close by caused the levels of these growth-promoting substances to fall (Butler 1978; Kuhn 1978). Scientists who study parents' contributions to the development of their offspring conclude that close contact and interaction between the mother and the infant regulate hormones and enzymes critical to growth (Hofer, 1982). In fact, infant development researchers believe that the mother has a regulatory effect on the infant's physiology and that her presence and interaction with the baby are necessary for the optimal functioning of these systems (Hofer, 1978).

Physicians have long recognized a condition known as failure-to-thrive in infants who do not form con-

Close contact with mother enables baby to function at an optimal level.

sistent and predictable attachments to a caregiver. It seems that the young of each species have a critical level of nurturing that they need in order to thrive. What is the level of nurturing that human infants need? While the exact answer to this question is unknown and perhaps cannot be determined absolutely for each individual, a clue comes from the fact that human infants are meant to be a continuous contact species. Infant care patterns of human cultures also provide information. In more primitive cultures that do not have the "benefits" of parenting books and professional advisors, mothers carry their infants in slings during the day, share sleep with them at night, allow unrestricted breastfeeding, and give immediate nurturing responses to crying. This responsive relationship does not seem to create overly dependent children (Lozoff 1979). Infants in cultures which practice attachment parenting show advanced developmental skills as compared to infants from cultures with more restrained styles of parenting (Geber 1958).

Attachment parenting helps organize the baby. The newborn's behavior is disorganized. His movements are random and jerky. Most of the cues he gives his parents seem purposeless and hard to decode. His sleep-wake cycles are exhaustingly irregular. One of the goals of parenting in the early months is to organize or regulate the baby. Critics of the attachment style of parenting argue that it puts the baby in charge and promotes disorganization. Research shows the opposite is true. Attachment parenting not only takes the rigidity out of schedules and respects the individuality of the baby and parents; it also promotes organization within the baby.

In one study, newborns became disorganized if they were not allowed to suck on cue; their sleep/wake cycles were better organized if they were allowed to cue feed. Newborns given responsive care develop day/night organization more rapidly than newborns on a four-hour feeding schedule (Anderson 1977). The organizing effect of attachment parenting seems to be needed because the maternal factors that regulate fetal biorhythms are lost at birth. During the early postnatal months, reorganization takes place, based on parent-infant interactions. An interruption of the attachment style of care may result in the gradual emergence of less organized behavior (purposeless or hyperactive movements) because regulatory processes hidden within the mother-infant relationship have been withdrawn (Sander 1970).

I believe that the main benefit of organization is that it promotes the state of quiet alertness. A baby who is better organized will spend more time in this state, a time when he is very receptive to learning and interacting with the environment. During quiet alert, the infant's systems seem to work better. Researchers have found that the stability of the infant's physiological systems is related to the capacity for attentive behavior during awake periods (Emde and Harmon 1982).

The behavior state of quiet alertness or attentive stillness also gives parents better opportunities to interact with the baby. Studies have shown that there is a direct relationship between the percentage of time a newborn is in the quiet alert state and the degree of mother-infant attachment.

I have noticed that infants exhibit more rhythmic, fluid, purposeful movements when they receive attachment parenting. The attachment style of parenting leads to a certain harmony, a fluidity of action between infant and parents. It helps you "go with the flow" of your infant's needs and helps your infant "go with the flow" of your lifestyle. It seems that the mother directs the energy of the baby toward more purposeful behavior and thus acts as the baby's conservator of energy. Since attached infants cry less, they conserve and redirect this energy toward purposeful interaction that enhances growth and development. The organized infant thrives better. Babies who feel less secure spend more time crying or withdrawing from interaction by sleeping. They spend less time in quiet interaction and therefore profit less from stimulation from their environment. Nor do they bring out the best in their caregiving parents. They don't fit well.

Attachment parenting and cognitive development. The brain grows more during infancy than at any other time, doubling its volume and reaching approximately sixty percent of its adult size by one year. As the brain grows, nerve cells, called neurons, proliferate. They resemble miles of tangled electrical wires. The infant is born with much of this wiring unconnected. During the first year, these neurons grow larger, learn to work better, and connect up with each other to make circuits which enable baby to think and do more things.

Here's how these circuits work. Each neuron is composed of three parts: a set of branching nerves called dendrites receive a message and pass this message into the cell body of the neuron. This cell body processes and stores the message and may send out its own message through another set of nerves called an axon. The tips of the axon branch out like feelers attempting to make connections with other nerves. The connections between the nerves are called synapses. During development two important improvements are made in this system: first, the number of synapses between nerves increases and second, each neuron acquires a coating called myelin which helps the messages move faster and insulates the nerves, preventing short circuits.

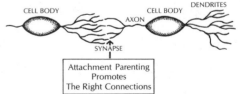

If nerve cells don't make connections they die. Researchers have shown that all parts of the nerve cell change size as a result of environmental input and that an enriched environment increases the weight of the brain in experimental animals

(Diamond 1984). For example, the infant sees mother or father's face. The nerves of the eyes transmit the image of the face to the area of the brain that processes visual information, and the infant stores the image of this face. Repeatedly seeing the face stimulates the infant to want to react; this requires some connections between nerves within the brain and to those leading out to the muscles. The infant's motor abilities develop from head to toe, so the earliest motor connections are to the face. Eventually, the stimulus of the parent's face causes the visual area of the brain to send a message to the motor area which controls the infant's facial muscles. The result is a smile. With continued neurological development, connections are made with other motor areas so that eventually baby can reach out and touch his mother or father's face with his hands and even later with his feet. The moral of this neurological story is that the more the infant has organized interaction with his environment, the more neurological connections he is able to develop.

Attachment parenting helps the infant's developing brain make the right connections. There are many studies on experimental animals that show that a secure mother-infant attachment and an appropriately responsive environment enhance brain development (Hofer 1982; Montagu 1971; Diamond 1984). Studies have shown that securely attached infants score higher on the Bayley Mental Development Index (Emde and Harmon 1982b). These researchers also found a positive relationship between securely attached infants and the development quotient (comparison of overall development to the norm), the quality of exploration in play, enthusiasm, persistence, the ability to use a caregiver for help with difficult tasks, and competence in interacting with a peer group. In his classic book *Touching*, Dr. Ashley Montagu theorizes that the human brain is purposely underdeveloped at birth so that the head is not too large to pass through the birth canal. He also presents evidence that the human infant needs a continued womb-like environment for an additional nine months in order to enhance brain development. In essence, attachment parenting feeds the brain with the right kind of stimulation at a time in the child's life when the brain needs the most nourishment.

Temperament refers to how your baby acts in certain circumstances or reacts to certain needs. It is important to understand that in the early months, your baby behaves the way he does primarily because of his inborn temperament, not because of your parenting abilities. Usually by the end of the first month parents can begin to see the type of personality that their baby has been blessed with. This leads to labels being applied to the baby. Some babies are labeled as easy babies. They are content in a variety of caregiving circumstances. They are somewhat consistent and predictable in their needs and adapt easily to a variety of schedules and parenting styles. Other babies, labeled difficult babies, may be super-sensitive to changes in their environment. These babies have intense needs and voice equally intense protests when those needs are not met. Their mothers may say things like "I just can't put her down" or "He wants to nurse all the time." These babies deservedly receive the label "demanding," but I prefer to call them "high need babies." Most babies' temperaments fall somewhere between these two extremes.

THE NEED LEVEL CONCEPT

NEED LEVEL OF BABY   PARENTING STYLE

Matching parenting style to the need level of the baby.

Your Infant's Temperament

I believe that babies come wired with a certain temperament for a reason. Every baby possesses a certain level of needs which must be filled if the baby is to develop to his maximum potential. It stands to reason that an infant would also come wired with some way of communicating his needs. This early language, mainly crying, is part of the infant's attachment-promoting behavior. An infant with a high level of needs also comes programmed with an intense way of communicating these needs. For example, babies who need a lot of holding in order to thrive will protest if they are put down.

Temperament matching. The temperament of the baby greatly affects the caregiving behavior of the parents. A good fit results when the need level of the baby matches the response level of the parents. Current research shows that the infant is not, as previously thought, a passive player in the parenting game, but rather is an active participant in shaping the parents' behavior, so that he can make himself understood. A mother of a high need baby once confided to me, "Our baby absolutely brings

TEMPERAMENT MATCHING

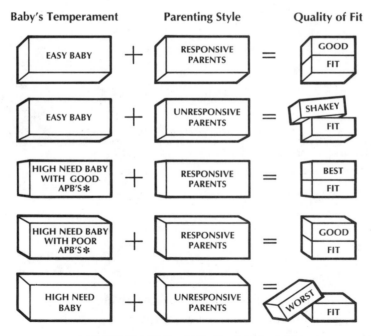

Baby's Temperament   Parenting Style   Quality of Fit

EASY BABY + RESPONSIVE PARENTS = GOOD FIT

EASY BABY + UNRESPONSIVE PARENTS = SHAKEY FIT

HIGH NEED BABY WITH GOOD APB'S✳ + RESPONSIVE PARENTS = BEST FIT

HIGH NEED BABY WITH POOR APB'S✳ + RESPONSIVE PARENTS = GOOD FIT

HIGH NEED BABY + UNRESPONSIVE PARENTS = WORST FIT

✳APB'S — ATTACHMENT PROMOTING BEHAVIORS

out the best and the worst in me." A parenting style that organizes the baby's temperament and increases the parents' sensitivity makes it possible to survive and thrive with a high need baby or with an easy baby. A good fit between the temperament of the baby and the nurturing style of the parents helps make it easier.

An easy baby with a responsive mother is a combination that will result in a good fit. Because mothers tend to feel that the "goodness" of their babies reflects their effectiveness as mothers, the mother in this case is likely to be delighted with the fit. Because easy babies are less demanding they do not always initiate interactions with their caregivers, but a responsive mother makes up for this by taking great care to invoke responses from the baby. This is why this is a good fit.

An easy baby with a more restrained mother is at a greater risk for attachment problems. Because the easy baby is not very demanding a less responsive mother may expend relatively little effort developing her mothering skills. She may feel that the baby doesn't seem to need her much and may seek more challenging activities elsewhere. In this match, not only does the mother fail to bring out the best in the baby, but the baby also does not bring out the best in the mother.

A high need baby with a responsive mother is a good match; both are likely to bring out the best in each other. A high need baby who has poor attachment-promoting skills especially needs a responsive mother. These babies, often known as non-cuddlers, are slow to warm up to caregiving. They appear not to need a lot of nurturing, but in reality they do. Parenting these babies may be difficult initially because the parents do not receive the appreciative signals they would get from a more cuddly baby who obviously enjoys being held and cared for. With a responsive mother, this baby usually does well. The mother does her best to initiate interaction and help the baby develop attachment-promoting skills. These babies need the best responses a parent can give in order for the best in themselves to develop.

The high need baby and the caregiver who consistently restrains her responses are at the highest risk for not developing a good fit. Neither one brings out the best in each other because the baby's language and needs are not understood.

What About Spoiling?

Parents have been led to believe that the practices which make up attachment parenting may spoil the infant and keep him from learning to be independent. Attachment parenting does not mean overindulgence or inappropriate dependency. The possessive parent or the "hover mother" is one who keeps an infant from doing what he needs to do because of her own needs. This has a detrimental effect on the development of both infant and parent. Attachment differs from dependency. Attachment enhances development; dependency may hinder it. Parents will be happy to know that current research has finally put the spoiling theories on the shelf—to spoil. Infants of the attachment style of parenting actually turn out to be sensitive children who are much easier to discipline. As one sensitive mother of a well-disciplined child proudly exclaimed, "He's not spoiled, he's perfectly fresh."

The Pay-Off

Upon first glance you may consider the attachment style of parenting to be all giving, giving, giving. To a certain extent it is. Babies are takers and parents are givers; that is a fact of parenting during the early months. However, there is another side to the parenting equation. The more the parents give to the baby, the more the baby gives back to the parents. Mutual giving leads to a mutual shaping of each other that helps all members of the family fit together. For example, when a mother breastfeeds her baby, holds and caresses him, or responds to his cry, she gives him both nourishment and comfort. The baby, in turn, gives something back to the mother. Sucking causes the mother to produce a hormone called prolactin. This hormone perhaps may be the biological basis for mothering behavior. Baby stimulates the mother to produce the very hormone which helps her to mother him intuitively. Baby indirectly plays an important part in his own care by boosting the mother's ability to care for him. This mutual giving is beautifully illustrated when a mother breastfeeds an infant off to sleep. (I call this "nursing down".) Mother gives her milk, which hap-

Mutual Giving

pens to contain a sleep-inducing substance (Graf 1984). Meanwhile, as mother suckles her baby, this sucking stimulates the mother's body to produce more prolactin, which has a tranquilizing effect on the mother. The mother helps put the baby to sleep, and the baby helps put the mother to sleep, a beautiful biological example of how mutual giving helps mothers and babies fit together.

Baby brings up the parents. The prominent infant psychologist Eric Erikson said, "A family can bring up a baby only by being brought up by him" (Erikson 1968). The mutual shaping of behavior by parents and infant is well illustrated in the development of communication. Baby's early communication is a language of needs. Crying and smiling are the two main tools used by the infant to communicate needs and reinforce responses to them. Parents gradually learn the language of baby's needs. On the surface they appear to undergo a regression to the level of the baby. They act, talk, and think down at the baby's level. The family first learns to respond to the language of the baby, but eventually the baby learns to speak the language of the family—after he has trained the family in the subtle art of non-verbal communication. The baby then learns to act, talk, and think at the parent's level. In other words, the parents first become like the baby in order that the baby can more easily become like the parents, and both develop communication skills that neither had before. Infant development researchers consider this phenomenon of mutual shaping one of the most important aspects of developing the fit (Anthony 1984).

The effect of the attachment style of parenting on parent and infant development may be summed up by one word—sensitivity. The infant and parents become mutually sensitive to one another. While studying parents and infants in preparation for this book I noticed the beneficial effect of the attachment

Mutual Giving

style of parenting on all aspects of parent and infant development. The most noteworthy effect was mutual sensitivity.

SUMMARY: *EFFECT OF PARENTING STYLE ON DEVELOPMENT*

The style

- Bonding at birth.
- Breastfeed with infant-led weaning.
- "Wear" your baby.
- Cries receive nurturing responses.
- Share sleep.
- Be open to your baby's needs.
- Respond to baby's cues.
- Involved father.

Effect on infant

- Enhances physical and intellectual growth.
- Promotes organization of behavior.
- Builds language and social skills.
- Smooths transitions between developmental stages.
- Helps develop a healthy sleep attitude.
- Discipline is easier.
- Child has feeling of rightness.
- Child learns to be independent.

Effect on parents

- Builds sensitivity.
- Increases powers of observation.
- Enhances intuitive responsiveness.
- Higher levels of mothering hormones.
- Better knowledge of baby's competencies and preferences.
- Better understanding of baby's temperament.
- More appropriate interactions with baby.
- Parents enjoy baby more.
- Matures marriage.
- Parents become more effective disciplinarians.

Effect on fit

- Establishes mutual giving.
- Mutual skill reinforcement.
- Mutual sensitivity.
- Everyone enjoys one another.
- Good communication.
- Healthy attachments and separations.

CHAPTER TWO:

What Parents Should Know About Infant Development

This chapter contains a discussion of the most important and interesting features of infant development which parents should be aware of as they both study and enjoy their infant through the first twelve months.

How a Baby Grows

There are two types of infant growth and development standards used by physicians and scientists. One measures physical growth, the other mental, motor, and social development. I call these "getting bigger" and "getting smarter" charts.

"GETTING BIGGER" CHARTS

There are a variety of charts available on which to plot the height, weight, and sometimes head growth of the child from birth to adolescence. The growth charts most widely used are the NCHS charts, derived from data obtained from the National Center for Health Statistics in 1976. These charts represent a cross-sectional average of generally healthy children. There is no attempt to divide the children by nutritional status, breastfeeding or bottle-feeding, body type, or parenting styles. The growth patterns are grouped in percentiles from the fifth to the ninety-fifth. This means that out of one hundred children fifty will be below the fiftieth percentile and fifty will be above. These charts are useful reference standards which serve to alert health care professionals to possible growth problems. It is important for parents to realize that these charts represent averages. Average growth is not the same as normal growth; there are wide variations in what is normal. Remember that your child is an individual.

"GETTING SMARTER" CHARTS

Growth means not only getting bigger in size but also increasing in behavioral competence. There are developmental charts that show the average age at which infants perform certain easily identifiable behaviors, such as sitting alone or walking. These behaviors are called developmental milestones. For example, the most widely used developmental chart, the Denver Developmental Screening Test (DDST) shows that fifty percent of infants walk at one year of age, but it also shows that there is a wide range of ages at which infants begin to walk.

Progression is more important than timing. Every normal child moves through an orderly sequence of developmental milestones. He will progress from sitting to pulling up to standing to walking. Different children may accomplish these motor milestones at different ages but they will all follow the same progression. *When* your child accomplishes these feats is not so important, but it *is* important that each month his skills progress in comparison with the previous month. Putting it in the terms of the elevator analogy, you could say that infants spend different amounts of time at each floor before moving on to the next higher floor. Some infants seem to make a quick stop at a floor and then quickly progress to the next. Some seem to skip some floors entirely. For example, while most infants crawl for some time before pulling themselves up and standing, others skip the crawling stage and scoot themselves across the room to pull up on a piece of furniture to stand. Both ways are normal. In the infants I have observed, I have noticed that the attachment style of parenting has more of an effect on smoothing out the progression through developmental milestones than it does on the actual timing.

Researchers have found that a secure parent-infant attachment and the use of social interactions to reinforce behavior accelerate the time it takes for an infant to progress from one milestone to the next, for example, going from standing alone to walking. They believe that the secure attachment contributes to the freeing of tension in the muscle groups which inhibit a given motor skill. This energy is diverted toward muscles which facilitate the skill (Kestenberg and Buelte 1983).

FACTORS AFFECTING GROWTH AND DEVELOPMENT CHARTS

Body type. There are three general body types, and each one has a different growth pattern. Ectomorph children are tall and slim with less prominent musculature and less fat. Endomorph children are the opposite, usually short and wide with a larger, shorter bone structure, large accumulations of fat around the trunk and thighs, and a generally round appearance. Mesomorph children are in between these other two body types. They have a more muscular, squared-off appearance and are generally described as broad. Children with these three body types will naturally follow different curves on the growth charts. Ectomorphs will be at a higher percentile in height and will be relatively low in weight; endomorphs will be the reverse. Both curves may be normal for the individual body type.

Health and nutrition. An illness such as a cold or diarrhea may be reflected in a temporary leveling-off of a child's growth, followed by a catch-up spurt. Predominantly breastfed babies may show a different growth pattern than predominantly bottle-fed infants. Studies are currently underway suggesting that breastfed babies do indeed show different growth patterns. Some infants show a smooth, steady increase in height and weight over the first year. Others show a start-and-stop pattern with periodic growth spurts followed by a leveling-off, followed by another spurt.

Central nervous system maturation. The infant develops from head to toe and from trunk to extremities. The infant's body develops this way because his brain does. An infant masters control of his head before his legs and his arms before his fingers. He uses his hands proficiently before standing on his feet. What a beautiful design! Consider how frustrated the infant would be if he could walk all over the room but could not pick up the things he saw. Brain centers for different behavioral skills such as vision, language, and expression of emotions develop at different ages. A skill seems to develop at a certain age mainly because the brain center for that skill matures at that time.

Temperament of the baby. Another factor affecting infant development is the personality of the individual baby. Impulsive, active, "tight" babies often are quicker to attain gross motor milestones (such as rolling over or twisting out of an infant seat) than more placid babies. Both kinds of babies are normal.

Parenting style. The way a caregiver responds to the cues of the infant can also affect development. As discussed in the previous chapter, attachment parenting helps babies to fulfil their potential.

The Five Areas of Development

Developmental skills can be grouped into five general areas: gross motor skills, fine motor skills, language, social skills, and cognitive skills.

GROSS MOTOR SKILLS

Gross motor behavior refers to how the infant uses his limb, trunk, and neck muscles—the larger muscles in his body. It includes such things as controlling his head, sitting, crawling, and walking. The development of baby's gross motor skills from birth to one year consists basically of getting more and more of his body off the ground, starting with the head and moving down his body. When lying on his tummy he first lifts his head off the ground, then his chest and abdomen. He gets his hips up off the ground in order to crawl, and then finally stands upright and walks on his legs.

FINE MOTOR SKILLS

Fine motor behavior includes the hand and finger skills which the infant uses to manipulate objects.

As with gross motor skills, development of fine motor skills follows an orderly progression, from imprecise punch-like reaching to an elegant pincer movement of the thumb and index finger which can pick up and put down the tiniest of objects.

LANGUAGE SKILLS

Language behavior includes both the sounds and the gestures which the infant uses to communicate with others. The progression of language development is much more variable and less easily identified than that of motor development. This area is the only one which absolutely requires interaction with another human being in order to develop optimally.

Parents can affect the development of their infant's language more than they can any other skill. The first year is often called the prelinguistic stage of language development; the infant learns to communicate before he is able to say words. For example, by using his first tool for communication, the cry, baby learns that language is a social interchange and that he can use signals to call for attention and get help. Appropriate responses from his caregivers help him to refine these primitive, demanding signals into more polite requests that are easier on the nerves.

Mothers are naturals at teaching their infants to speak, developing a dialogue style called "motherese" which is universal. Mothers show a natural sensitivity in respecting their infant's language competence. They do not demand responses above the infant's level of competence, yet they are able to shift to a higher level of communication when the infant is ready. The attachment style of parenting greatly enhances language development because it helps parents tune in and respond to the infant's language and cues. Better responses motivate babies to refine their language skills.

SOCIAL AND PLAY BEHAVIOR

Social and play behavior includes the infant's inter-actions with caregivers, objects, and toys in his environment. At first, a baby's social interactions are simple and limited. They usually revolve around feeding. As baby is able to see and remember faces he learns to recognize his parents and to distinguish them from strangers. His best smiles and most play-ful interactions will be reserved for them. When parents respond to their baby's initial social over-tures, they encourage him to be even more sociable and to trust his caregiving environment.

COGNITIVE DEVELOPMENT

"I wonder what my baby is thinking." Trying to see inside a baby's mind is a common pastime of new parents. Cognitive growth is the most elusive fea-ture of infant development. You will never truly know what your child is thinking until he is several years old and is able to tell you (and even then, his reasoning may be very different from yours). Because babies cannot tell us what they are think-ing, researchers and parents must deduce what the infant is thinking from his actions.

Cognitive skills include the ability to think, to rea-son, to make adjustments to different situations, and to solve the problems created by rapid develop-ment. Using these abilities develops intelligence. One of the newest ideas about infant cognitive development, one not appreciated by earlier researchers, is that sensitive and responsive caregivers can have a profound effect on intellectual development.

The five areas of infant development (gross motor, fine motor, language, social, and cognitive) are inter-related. Cognitive development is a result of the development of other areas and in turn, affects their further maturation. For example, increasing central nervous system maturation allows the eyes to focus on objects a few feet away and the arms to reach

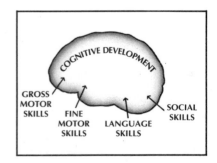

out and grab. As a result, the infant is faced with a primitive type of decision as to what to do with the toy in his hands; he has to think about the toy. The mental processes that prompt him to study a toy in one hand, transfer it to the other, or gather it in toward his mouth (this last usually seems more automatic than cognitive) stimulate the refinement of the visual-motor skills needed to perform these various manipulations.

How the Infant Develops Competence

Competence comes with the development of abilities. An infant develops locomotor competence when he can get from one place to another first by crawling and then by walking. Most infant competencies are the result not only of the infant's inborn abilities, but also of the ways in which the caregiving environment has helped him develop. For example, the development of social competence, the ability to enlist the help of others, depends a great deal on how responsive the caregivers are to the infant's cues for assistance. It may therefore be more accurate to discuss the competencies of the parent-infant pair rather than to focus on the infant alone. This is what I have tried to do in this book.

If a highly competent infant is paired with a less sensitive, less responsive mother, he is less likely to develop his social competence to its fullest potential. If a less competent infant is paired with a highly responsive mother, the infant is likely to improve his competencies. A highly competent infant paired with a highly responsive mother is likely to result in both members of the pair developing their social competence to the fullest potential. The influence of mothers on the development of social competence in their infants was well illustrated in an experiment by Bell and Ainsworth (1973). These researchers examined the mother's responsiveness to her infant's crying and the infant's later development of communication skills. They found that when mothers responded promptly to their infant's crying, the babies developed better communication skills toward the end of the first year—they were more socially competent. Researchers feel that the development of social competence may have a carry-over effect on other skills because it fosters an overall feeling of confidence.

PARENTING STYLE AND COMPETENCE

Studies have shown that parenting style can have a significant influence on the infant's I.Q. (Ainsworth and Bell 1974; Beckwith 1971). The following factors, listed in order of importance, were shown to exert a positive effect: maternal responsiveness to the infant's signals; high maternal verbal and physical contact with the infant; acceptance of and going along with the infant's temperament; permitting the baby to have freedom of movement to explore the world; and providing a stimulating environment of toys and play activities which encourage decision-making and problem-solving. Those factors which negatively influenced an infant's I.Q. were lack of maternal verbal and physical contact, many restrictions on exploration, and frequent punishment. It is interesting that parental education was not significantly correlated with I.Q. in the infants studied at eight and eleven months. This supports the idea that, at least in the early years, parents' ability to nurture is more important to their children than intellectual accomplishments.

A sensitive, nurturing environment teaches baby to trust.

The Pay-Off

I believe that the most important effect of parenting style on development is that babies who are the products of a sensitive and nurturing environment learn that the world is a nurturing place to be and that people nurture people. In adult jargon we call this a mindset. These babies learn to relate to people more than things. They become high-touch children in a high-tech world. The high-touch infant has learned to be intimate with others. He is capable of strong attachments, because he uses the mindset he has learned from his attachment to his parents as the standard to measure all future attachments. In essence, this infant has learned to give and receive love.

CHAPTER THREE: THE FIRST MONTH

Getting Started

The first minutes, hours, days of a baby's life are very exciting ones for parents. Finally you get to meet the baby you've wondered and dreamed about all through pregnancy. Getting off to a good start at parenting means knowing what to expect and planning for a birth experience that allows the whole family—mother, father, and baby—to be together as much as possible during this very sensitive time.

Your Baby's Birth

A safe and healthy entry into the world. The first two minutes after birth are of critical importance to the health of the newborn. Amazing changes occur in baby's lungs and circulatory system to allow immediate adaptation to life outside the womb. The collapsed lungs suddenly fill with air and the breathing mechanism automatically clicks in. As the umbilical cord is clamped and cut, baby's circulatory system adapts by automatically closing off the blood vessels that connected the baby to the placenta and opening up new ones to the lungs. Some babies need temporary medical assistance to make this transition. Some gentle stimulation or a few minutes of oxygen will help him "pink up." Excess mucusy fluid may need to be suctioned from his mouth. Babies may remain mucusy for several days after birth.

First meeting. How a mother and baby get started with each other sets the tone for how quickly they get to know one another. Because newborns get cold easily, many hospitals place new babies in mechanically warmed bassinettes immediately after birth. Unless there are medical complications, mother's body makes a far better "warmer." Immediately after delivery, the baby should be placed skin-to-skin on the mother's abdomen, his head nestling between her breasts. The baby's back and head should be covered with a warm towel. This is not just good psychology; it is also good medicine. Imagine what a warm, snuggly place is this first home. Draping baby over mother, tummy to tummy, cheek to breast, allows for a natural heat transfer from mother to baby.

The first hour after birth is a prime time of receptivity for mother and infant, a period in which both mother and newborn are programmed to be sensitive to each other. Within minutes after birth the

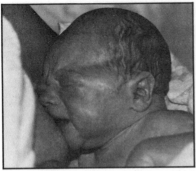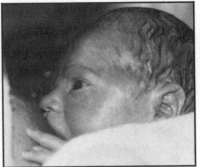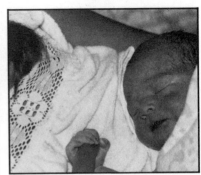

First meeting between mother and baby: distress is followed by comfort.

newborn enters a state of **quiet alertness**, the state in which he is most able to interact with his environment. During this alert stage baby looks directly into mother's eyes and snuggles at her breast. Mother and baby have a mutual need for each other; the baby needs to be with his mother and the mother needs to be with her baby. The baby feels content as his body molds to match the contours of mother's warm chest and abdomen. During this first meeting the baby is relatively still. Perhaps he is so enthralled by what he sees, hears, and feels that he doesn't want to waste any energy by squirming. The baby drinks in the sound of mother's voice, the feel of her warm skin, and the taste of her milk. The baby suckles while mother continues to soothe him. Both feel right. The baby knows that he belongs. A bond is formed between him and his parents. Usually within an hour or two after birth, the baby drifts contentedly into a deep sleep.

Your baby learns a very important lesson during this first meeting. He learns that distress is followed by comfort. This helps him develop the single most valuable quality he needs in order to grow into a secure child and adult—the ability to trust his environment.

Here is a tip that gets a new family off to a good start. After the attending medical personnel have done their jobs ("after the dust has settled," as one

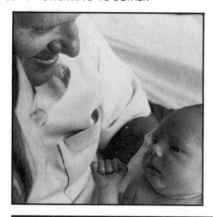

father put it) and mother and baby are well, request some private time to be together, mother, father, and baby. You, as parents, can revel in the joy of finally seeing and holding the product of your love. This special time of family intimacy should not be interrupted by trivial hospital routines. Mother and baby should receive a minimum of medication so that they can both be awake and aware and able to enjoy this special time.

BIRTHDAY PICTURES

Some writers have described the newly born baby as looking like a prize fighter—after the fight. But as you examine your baby in the first hour after birth, you, his parents, will probably find him beautiful.

Baby's puffy face and eyelids are the result of extra fluid accumulated beneath the skin. He will show some signs of having to squeeze a bit to enter the world. His red face has areas of bluish purple, dotted with freckled spots from tiny broken blood vessels. Several other characteristics of the face and head give further evidence of the baby's tight squeeze through the birth canal: a flattened nose, ears pressed against the head, and a slight bruising of the skin over the prominent cheek bones.

The watermelon shape of your baby's head is the result of a process called **molding**. This is necessary to help your baby's head fit through the pelvic bones during delivery. Molding protects the underlying brain. The top of your baby's skull is made up of five bones which are joined together by tough membranes. As your baby's head enters the birth canal, these bones move and allow the head to elongate to conform more easily to the changing shape of the birth canal. Because of the molding, your baby's head is larger and longer in the back, and his forehead is relatively flat. The skull bones may overlap a bit with the joints appearing like ridges, especially on the top and sides of baby's head. Molding is more noticeable after longer labors and in babies with larger heads. There is less molding in breech presentations, and it may not be present at all in babies delivered by cesarean.

You will feel a relatively soft area in the center top of your newborn's head where four of the bones join. This soft spot, called a fontanelle, is covered by a thick membrane. It will gradually get smaller as the bones in your baby's skull grow together. There is another smaller fontanelle toward the back of your baby's head along the midline. The soft spots are actually pretty tough. It's okay to touch them and wash them. Sometimes you'll see and be able to feel a pulse through the soft spot.

The scalp is usually swollen, especially near the front, also a result of squeezing during birth. This swelling is called a **caput**. The molding and scalp swelling usually disappear within a few days after birth. Occasionally tiny blood vessels beneath the scalp may break during delivery, allowing blood to accumulate and form a sort of "goose egg" on baby's scalp. This is called a **cephalohematoma**. These bumps may take several months to disappear and sometimes feel very hard as the underlying blood calcifies.

A fine silky baby hair, matted with amniotic fluid and specks of blood, covers your baby's head. You will also notice patches of fine furry hair, called **lanugo**, on baby's ear lobes, cheeks, shoulders, and upper back. This hair disappears in a few months.

Your newborn's beautiful skin is covered with a white, cheesy, slippery material called **vernix**, which protects it from the amniotic fluid and acts like a lubricant during vaginal delivery. You'll want your newborn covered with a towel and blotted dry, but don't be in a hurry to wipe off this protective coating. Vernix seems to protect the skin even after birth and need not be wiped off.

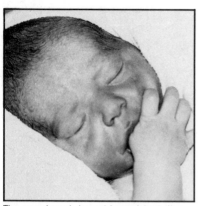

The newborn's head is molded, the face puffy.

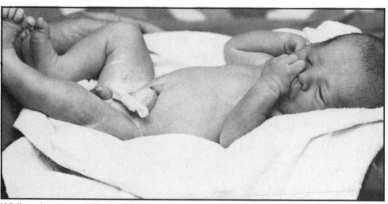

White, cheesy vernix covers the skin.

Your newborn's skin undergoes rapid changes. Some babies have smooth, tight-fitting skin, others (especially post-mature or small-for-date babies) have loose-fitting, wrinkled skin. There may be areas of cracking and peeling, especially on the abdomen, the front of the feet, the ankles, and in the various creases. You do not need to lubricate the cracked areas of baby's skin; his natural skin oils will do the job. The flaky, rough, cracked areas of your baby's skin will smooth out within a few weeks. Baby's skin also undergoes rapid color changes during the first hour and the first week, changing from reddish blue to cherry red to yellowish pink, as the blood cells and blood vessels adapt to postnatal life. You will notice fatty areas, called **fat folds**, on your baby's body, especially along the back of the neck, the cheeks, the sides of the nose, and underneath the arms. A large fat fold under the baby's recessed chin looks like a double chin and completely covers his short neck.

Baby's eyes. The eyes are the most captivating part of your newborn's face. Within moments after birth, newborns open their eyes in anticipation of meeting another pair of eyes. The puffy eyelids with the slit-like openings between them protect the sensitive newborn eyes from too much light too soon. The newborn also has an efficient blink reflex to protect him from light. This is why it's a good idea to dim the lights after delivery, to encourage the baby to keep his eyes wide open and gaze at his parents' faces. Newborns seldom keep their eyes wide open for very long. Their eyelids seem heavy. They have intermittent periods of visual alertness after which they drift off into stages of deepening sleep.

Sometimes the nerves which control the upper eyelids are squeezed during delivery, causing a temporary droopy eyelid. When your baby's eyes are wide open and searching for another pair of eyes, you may notice tiny broken blood vessels throughout the white parts of his eyes. These are a result of the delivery and will go away within a few weeks.

For the first few days, your newborn will assume a position similar to the one he was accustomed to *in utero*. The arms and legs flex toward the body in a frog-like position. The hands are usually drawn up toward the face; some newborns even begin caressing their faces within the first hours after birth, as if they had grown accustomed to this comforting practice in the womb. A newborn's fists are tightly clenched most of the time, and his bowed legs and turned-in feet are drawn up around his diaper.

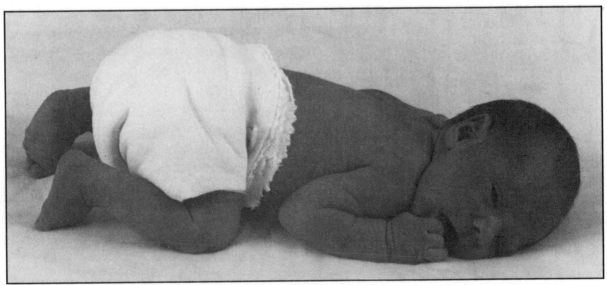

The newborn's arms and legs are flexed, as *in utero*.

Babies who have been in the breech position in the womb may not flex their knees; instead their legs will be bent upwards with their toes almost touching their heads.

Extra fluid often accumulates in the newborn's genitalia, resulting in a swollen appearance. The scrotum of the male and the labia of the female are normally swollen at birth because of this extra fluid.

Your baby's umbilical cord is soft and jelly-like. The clamp is placed an inch or so away from the base of the cord. Your health care provider will instruct you on the care of baby's umbilical cord.

Baby's vital statistics. The full-term newborn usually weighs between five-and-a-half and eight-and-a-half pounds (2.5 to 3.8 kg) and is between twenty and twenty-one and a half inches (50 to 54 cm) long. His head is proportionately large and about one-quarter of his total length. A newborn's heartbeat is twice as fast as an adult's: 120-130 beats per minute. He also breathes twice as fast as an adult, forty to fifty times per minute.

Soon after delivery, most birth attendants will score your newborn, a reminder that this is a world where science measures human beings quantitatively from the moment of birth. This initial scoring is called an **Apgar score**, a scale developed by Dr. Virginia Apgar nearly thirty years ago as a measure of the general condition of newborn babies. The Apgar scores, taken at one and five minutes after birth, are based on five parameters: skin color, breathing effort, heart rate, muscle tone, and activity. The infant is awarded zero, one, or two points in each area, with ten being a perfect score. I wish to offer a bit of caution to parents about Apgar scores. In reality most normal healthy newborns do not achieve a score of ten. It is usual for a baby's hands and feet to remain somewhat blue for a few hours after birth, as his circulatory system adjusts to life outside the womb. Also, many healthy newborns, especially those who have experienced relatively easy and natural births, do not cry much immediately after birth and therefore lose points for not "crying lustily." I believe that the state of quiet alertness is more desirable than crying, although this would not be reflected in a higher Apgar score. A baby who scores ten, therefore, is not necessarily healthier than a baby who scores seven or eight. The Apgar score given to parents after the routine delivery of a normal, healthy baby has very little predictive value. A low Apgar score should not be a source of anxiety. Its main function is to alert the attending medical personnel to observe the baby carefully over the next few hours.

Routine injections and medications. Soon after birth most newborns receive an injection of vitamin K which promotes normal blood clotting. Either silver nitrate or an antibiotic ointment is administered to baby's eyes to protect them against bacteria they may have encountered in the birth canal. Erythromycin ointment is preferred over silver nitrate which may have an irritating effect. Ideally these routine procedures are delayed until at least one hour after birth so that mother, father, and baby can spend some time together without outside interference.

FIRST FEELINGS

The baby you finally get to see at birth is the baby you have been getting to know all through pregnancy. I have noticed that new parents immediately regard their newborn as a person, a new member of the family. "He has your ears," mother may say to father. "She has her grandmother's toes," parents may exclaim. I have noticed that during this first meeting mothers and fathers first look at their newborns with a sort of wide angle lens, getting an overall picture of this new unique little person. Then they gradually shift their focus to their newborn's specific body parts. Within minutes after birth a physical and emotional bonding takes place.

Mother experiences the desire to see, touch, protect, comfort, and nurture this new person who was previously inside her womb and not so accessible. Mothers are reluctant to release their babies, wanting to hold their little ones as close as possible for as long as possible. They may feel that it would not be right for the baby to be separated from them for any length of time after having been so close to them during the nine months of pregnancy.

I remember the feelings I had at the birth of our sixth baby. I had the privilege of catching our baby. As I cut the cord I felt that I was enabling our new son, Matthew, and my wife, Martha, both to separate and then to quickly reunite, as they now shared their feeling of oneness in a different way. Birth brings a sense of completion as mother and baby meet one another face to face. The attachment begun during pregnancy continues; birth changes only the manner in which this attachment is expressed. Even in the first few minutes after birth parents will notice patterns of behavior in the baby, such as sucking their thumbs or touching their faces, patterns that must have begun in the womb. You will notice that you spend more time touching the face of your newborn than any other body part; this is part of the bonding process.

What about the baby who for some reason, such as prematurity or a cesarean delivery, is temporarily separated from his mother after birth? Is the baby permanently affected by the loss of this early contact? Bonding time at birth is not like instant glue which cements a mother-baby relationship forever. There are many steps which must be taken before a strong mother-infant attachment develops. Time spent together during this biologically sensitive period gives this attachment a head start, but a strong attachment begins to develop whenever mother and baby are reunited. This compensates for the loss of early contact.

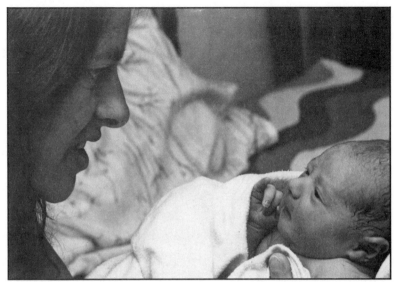

At birth, mother and baby separate, yet still feel a oneness.

Bonding with the father after cesarean births. If mother is unable to spend time with her baby immediately after birth because of a medical complication, the father should be invited to be with his baby in the delivery room and the newborn nursery. Studies have shown that at six months postpartum, fathers of infants delivered by cesarean were engaged in more caregiving activities, especially soothing the baby, than fathers of vaginally delivered infants. These studies suggest that extended early contact with the baby can bring out the best in fathers, too.

Let me share with you the story of Jim, a father whose wife recently had a cesarean birth. Jim, a big strapping macho type of man, wasn't sure he really wanted to get involved with the birth. After all, he thought, this whole scene was really a woman's thing and maybe he'd be better off in the waiting room until the drama was over. Nevertheless, I encouraged Jim to accompany me into the delivery suite to see his new baby. After I had performed my pediatrician's duties and was sure that the baby was warm, pink, and breathing well, I encouraged Jim to accompany the baby and me to the newborn nursery. Jim was still in awe of all the theatrics surrounding the operation, but he obediently followed me. After I placed his baby in the infant warmer, I said to him, "Jim, I need to attend another delivery. It's necessary that someone stay with your baby and stimulate him, because babies breathe better when someone is stroking them and talking to them." I encouraged Jim to get his hands on the baby and talk and sing to him and rub his back and just let himself be as loving and as caring as he could. When I returned, I congratulated Jim for stroking, touching, and singing to his baby and assured him that his initial investment was going to pay long-term dividends. The next day, when I made my hospital rounds and went in to talk with Jim's wife, she exclaimed, "What on earth happened to my husband? I can't get our baby away from him. He's really hooked. I never thought I'd see that big guy so sensitive."

First Days

Bonding does not end in the delivery room. It begins there. Unless prevented by a medical complication, healthy mothers and healthy babies should be together in the hospital from the time of birth to discharge. Today's hospitals and birthing centers offer a variety of newborn care options, from total nursery care (baby is primarily cared for by nursery nurses and brought to mother at scheduled times), to modified or full rooming-in where the baby stays in the mother's room some or all of the time.

I strongly advise mothers to have their babies room-in with them. All babies are born with attachment-promoting qualities—features and behaviors designed to alert the caregiver of the baby's presence and draw him or her, magnet-like, toward the baby. These features include the roundness of the baby's eyes, cheeks, and body, the softness of his skin, the smell of his skin, and, most important of all, baby's early language—his cries. These irresistible features make you want to hold and cuddle your baby. Having your baby with you in the hospital allows these attachment-promoting qualities to work in the way they were designed to work.

First sounds. A baby's cry is designed to help the baby survive and to develop the mother's caretaking behavior. The opening sounds of the baby's cry are designed to activate or release a mother's emotions. When she hears her baby cry the flow of blood to a mother's breasts increases and she feels a biological urge to pick up and nurse her baby. The baby's signals trigger a physical, hormonal response in the mother. No other signal can trigger such intense emotion in a mother as her baby's cry. At no other time in a child's life will his language so forcefully stimulate the mother to act.

When babies and mothers room-in together, they begin to understand each other from the start. When the baby begins to cry, the mother, because she is there and attuned to the baby, immediately picks him up and nurses him. The baby stops crying. The next time the baby awakens, squirms, grimaces, and cries, mother's response is the same. Soon the mother notices her baby's opening cues— waking, squirming, grimacing—and she picks up and nurses him *before* he begins to cry. Mother has learned to read her baby's pre-cry signals and responds appropriately. After rehearsing this interchange many times during a hospital stay, mother and baby feel confident about their ability to understand one another. Baby learns to give better cues, and a mother learns to respond better. Harmony develops between mother and baby when they room-in together, and this harmony helps mother and baby become more competent at interacting with one another.

Rooming-in helps mother and baby develop harmony.

Contrast this rooming-in scene with what goes on in a hospital nursery. A baby's cry has two phases. The early sound has an attachment-promoting quality, but if the cry goes unanswered, the later sounds are more disturbing and may promote avoidance. Picture the newborn infant lying in a plastic box. He awakens because he's hungry, and he cries, along with twenty other hungry babies who have all managed to awaken each other. A nurse who is kind and caring but has no biological attachment to the baby—no inner receiver tuned to that baby—hears the early attachment-promoting cries and responds as soon as time permits. The crying, hungry baby is taken to the mother, but with little urgency. The mother, meanwhile, has missed the opening scene in the biological drama because she was not present in the nursery when her baby first cried. But she is expected to give a nurturing response to a baby who by this time has either given up crying and fallen asleep or is "over the hill" on the crying curve and is now greeting the mother with more intense, disturbing cries. The mother, who has the biological attachment to the baby, hears only the cries that are likely to elicit more agitated concern or even an avoidance response. So even though she has a comforting breast to offer the baby, she is so tied up in knots her milk won't let down, and the baby cries even harder and is too worked up to latch on and nurse. The mother feels inadequate because she hasn't been able to comfort her baby, and so the baby winds up spending even more time in the nursery. This leads to more missed cues and more missed opportunities for taking advantage of attachment-promoting behavior. Mother and baby leave the hospital together, but they are still strangers.

How different things are for the rooming-in baby. He awakens in his mother's room, maybe in her arms. His pre-cry signals are promptly attended to, and he is put to the breast before he needs to cry. If the baby does cry, it is the initial attachment-promoting cry, and when given a prompt nurturing response, it never has a chance to develop into a disturbing cry. The attachment-promoting cries elicit a hormonal response in the mother, her milk lets down, and the mother and infant are in biological harmony.

Speaking as a former director of a university hospital's newborn nursery, I would say that nursery babies cry harder, but rooming-in babies cry better. Mothers and babies really do profit from rooming-in together: the infants cry less, the mothers exhibit more developed coping skills. The infant distress syndrome—fussiness, colic, incessant crying—is more common in infants kept in a central nursery than in babies who room-in with their mothers.

An infant needs to fit into his environment, to feel that he can be understood and know to whom he belongs. A baby who fits, feels right. A baby who feels right, acts right and is more of a joy to parent. Rooming-in leads to fitting in. When mother and baby fit well together, they bring out the best in each other.

How Your Newborn Changes

Babies change almost before your eyes. Watching babies grow and mature is the most rewarding aspect of caring for them. Many exciting physical changes take place already within the first month.

NORMAL BABY MARKS

Nearly all newborns have smooth reddish-pink dot-like marks that are most prominent on the upper eyelids, the forehead between the eyes, and the nape of the neck. These "stork bites" are areas where the blood vessels are prominent and show through a newborn's thin skin. They are called nevi (nevus means birthmark) and nearly always fade and disappear with time. The small, reddish patch just above the bridge of the baby's nose is often the first to fade, followed by the upper eyelid nevi, and then the nevi on the nape of the neck, although this may persist and eventually be covered by hair.

Another type of birthmark is called the strawberry nevus because of its bright red bubbly appearance. This type of nevus is seldom present at birth but appears a few days to weeks later, gradually increasing in size. It may take as long as several years for it to disappear completely.

Mongolian blue spots are bruise-like marks on the lower back and buttocks. These marks are very common in Asian, Indian, and black babies. They often fade with time, but many never disappear completely. It is important for health care providers and others to recognize that mongolian spots are common and normal and not signs of child abuse.

Rashes. Erythema toxicum is a common rash that appears within the first week. It consists of multiple red splotches smaller than a dime with slightly raised yellow pimply centers. It disappears in a week and needs no treatment.

Milia

Most newborns have tiny, whitish, pin-head bumps called milia (milk spots) which are most prominent on the nose. Milia are caused by plugged skin pores, and with gentle washing they will disappear within a few weeks. During the second week or later, newborn skin may appear oily and pimply, a condition resembling teen-age acne. Like teen-age acne, these pimples are caused by hormones which are still at high levels from birth. The hormones cause the oil glands in the skin to distend with retained secretions. This facial acne disappears with gentle washing with warm water. A similar acne-like crusty rash, called seborrhea, may appear over the scalp and behind the ears. A prescription cream in addition to normal washing may be needed to remove the rash completely.

Babies' scalps are especially prone to a flaky, dandruff-like condition called cradle cap. When mild, this needs no more than an occasional gentle washing. Scrubbing the scalp with soap too vigorously or too often may dry the skin and cause the cradle cap to worsen. Occasionally cradle cap becomes oily, crusty, and plaque-like, especially over baby's soft spot. To remove it, massage vegetable oil into the crusty area and then gently comb out the softened scales with a fine-toothed comb or soft brush. If cradle cap persists, your doctor may prescribe a cream and a tar shampoo. These crusty rashes are worse in the wintertime because of the dry air caused by central heating. A humidifier in baby's bedroom should help.

Prickly heat is another common newborn rash. It appears as tiny clear pimples on a red base in areas of the skin where there is excessive heat and moisture retention, such as in the folds of the neck, behind the ears, or on areas of the trunk covered by tight-fitting clothing. Prickly heat is best controlled by dressing baby in lighter weight, loose-fitting clothing. Gentle baths in cool water with an added tablespoon of baking soda will also help.

BABY'S BREATHING PATTERNS

When watching your sleeping baby breathe, you will notice an irregular pattern. He appears to stop breathing periodically, sometimes for as long as ten to fifteen seconds, and then starts again without any apparent problems. This is called periodic breathing and is normal for the tiny infant. The younger or more premature the baby, the more irregular the breathing pattern and the more noticeable the periodic breathing. Over the next few months, babies' breathing patterns become more regular, though they continue to breathe much faster than adults.

Besides being irregular breathers, newborns are also noisy breathers. They accumulate a lot of mucus or saliva in the backs of their throats, causing a gurgly sound. Newborns are obligate nose breathers which means that they breathe through their noses much more easily than through their mouths. Because their nasal passages are narrow, even a slight amount of congestion can result in noisy breathing. Babies seldom breathe with their mouths open. Even when his mouth is open during sleep, a baby's tongue is curled up to the roof of his mouth. This makes it difficult for him to breathe through his mouth. Babies breathe better when placed on their stomachs with the head turned slightly to one side. This allows the tongue and any mucus in the throat to come forward making more room for air to pass.

CHANGES IN YOUR BABY'S DIAPERS

In the first few days, babies' stools are black, tar-like, and sticky. This substance is called meconium and is composed of amniotic fluid debris from the intestines. Over the next few days, the stools become less sticky and greenish-brown. Between one and two weeks, they take on a yellowish color and a more regular consistency. The stools of breast-feeding babies are yellow, seedy, with a mustard-like consistency and a not unpleasant buttermilk-like odor. The changes in a breastfed baby's stools give a clue to the changes in the mother's milk; as the milk comes in and the amount of fat in it increases, the stools become more yellow and mustard-like. Because breast milk has a natural laxative effect, the stools of breastfed babies are more frequent and softer than the stools of formula-fed babies, which tend to be firmer and darker with an unpleasant odor. Added iron in the formula makes the stools greenish. The number of stools varies greatly in newborns. Some babies will have a loose stool after every breastfeeding. A newborn who is getting a sufficient amount of breast milk will have two to five bowel movements a day. Mothers often hear the gurgly sound of a soft stool a few minutes into a

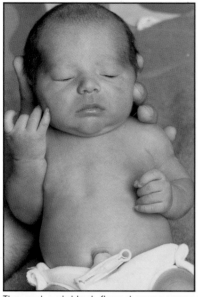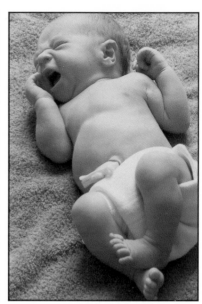

The red, wrinkled, flexed appearance of the newborn.

THE NEWBORN

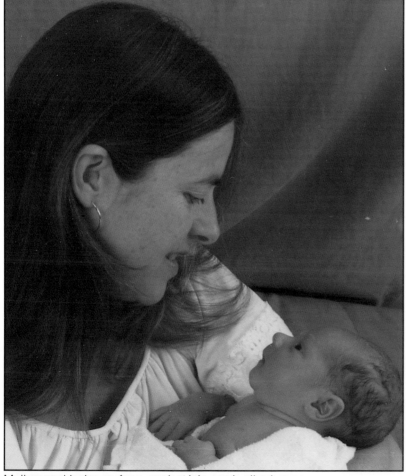

Mother and baby *en face*, gazing into each other's eyes.

Sharing sleep

"Wear" your baby.

Watch for baby's cues.

Bonding at birth

ATTACHMENT PARENTING

Respond to crying

Breastfeed with infant-led weaning

Father involvement at birth . . .

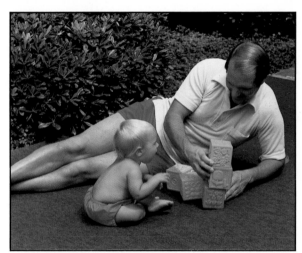

. . .and throughout the first year.

The pay-off: a baby who trusts and who feels right

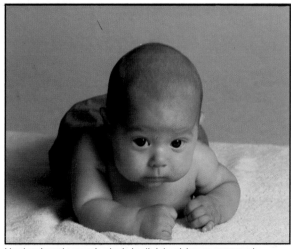

Understand your baby's individual temperament.

The neck nestle

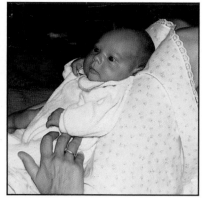

Sitting up on mother's legs

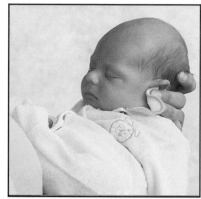

Bent and facing dad

Front carrier

Colic carry—helps relieve gassiness

Riding on mother's hip

Bent at the hips and facing forward

Nestling in the baby sling

HOLDING PATTERNS

You'll discover lots of ways to hold and comfort your new baby.
Here are just a few examples.

feeding. While the stools of a newborn baby are usually mustard-yellow, an occasional green stool is of no consequence if baby seems generally well. Occasionally some babies will have a hard stool or a sudden explosive stool that causes a tiny tear in baby's rectum, called a rectal fissure. This will result in a few spots of bright red blood on baby's diaper or streaks of blood in the stools. Fissures usually heal easily; lubricating baby's rectum with pediatric glycerine suppositories, as advised by your doctor, can help.

The urine of newborn babies is very unconcentrated and water-like and may take on a yellow-amber color only after a few weeks. It is common for newborns to have only two or three wet diapers during the first few days. Thereafter a newborn should wet at least six to eight cloth diapers (four to five disposables) each day. Newborns may actually urinate as many as twenty times a day.

THE UMBILICAL CORD

Babies' umbilical cords are usually cut and clamped about one inch away from their bodies. At first your baby's cord may be swollen. You may be able to see the blood vessels beneath the jelly-like transparent skin. Over the first two days of life, baby's umbilical cord shrivels up and dries, but it may not completely detach for a week or two. It is important to keep the area around the cord clean and dry, using a cotton-tipped applicator and alcohol. This cleaning routine should continue for a few days after the cord falls off, until the area is completely dry. It is normal to notice a few drops of blood the day the cord falls off.

FINGERNAILS AND TOENAILS

Babies' fingernails and toenails are fully formed at birth. Sometimes the fingernails are so long (especially in post-mature babies) that they need to be cut right away to prevent babies from scratching their faces. It is easiest to trim a baby's fingernails while he is asleep. Or you can gently bite them off while the baby is nursing. Newborn babies' toenails do not seem to grow as fast. They often appear to be ingrown into the skin on the sides of the toes, but because they are so soft and flexible, this usually is not a problem.

NEWBORN PUBERTY

During the first week or two, the excess maternal hormones that cross the placenta into the baby's blood stream during pregnancy may give rise to changes resembling the onset of puberty. Around the second or third week, or sooner, you may notice that the baby's breasts are enlarged (both male and female babies show this) and may even be secreting a few drops of milk. This is a normal response and will subside within a few weeks. Sometimes a newborn girl may have a few drops of blood coming from the vagina resembling a menstrual period. This is also normal.

WEIGHT CHANGES

Newborns will usually lose between five and eight percent of their birth weight (six to ten ounces) during the first week. Babies are born with extra fluid and fat to tide them over until their mothers' milk can supply sufficient fluid and nutrition. There are several factors that affect the amount of weight a baby loses. Large babies who have a lot of extra fluid tend to lose more weight. Their skin may feel more wrinkled as they lose this extra fluid during the first week. Babies who room-in with their mothers and are breastfed on cue tend to lose the least weight, if any at all. Babies born at home will usually lose less weight than babies born in a hospital. I feel this is not because of the location of the baby's birth, but rather the fact that home birth and rooming-in babies are not separated from their mothers and therefore tend to nurse more often. Another factor influencing the amount of weight loss during the first week is how soon the mother's milk comes in. Babies who are with their mothers constantly and can breastfeed frequently tend to lose less weight because the milk comes in sooner, giving them a higher-calorie milk as well as more of it. Babies who are separated from their mothers a lot during the first week or who are fed according to a schedule tend to lose the most weight. In addition to recording baby's birth weight, parents should remember to record baby's weight upon discharge from the hospital as this is an important reference for measuring weight gain at the first check-up two or three weeks later. Breastfed babies usually show a slower weight gain than formula-fed babies during the first two weeks; thereafter, breastfed babies and bottle-fed babies show similar weight gains, averaging around an ounce a day during the last two weeks of the first month. Most babies will gain an average of a pound to a pound and a half during the first month.

Another factor influencing your baby's weight gain is his body type. Ectomorph babies, recognized by their lean and lanky appearance, long fingers, and long, narrow feet, show a slower gain in weight and a proportionately greater increase in height than do babies who are mesomorphs (medium build) or endomorphs (short, pudgy hands and feet, and shorter, wider fingers and toes).

Newborn Reflexes

There are two types of actions: cognitive and reflexive. Cognitive means there is thought before the action. For example, when a baby is shown a rattle, the thinking part of his brain decides, "I'll use my hand to get the rattle," and the brain sends a message to the muscles, instructing them to grab the rattle. Reflexive actions are automatic. A familiar example is the knee jerk reflex. When your knee is tapped at just the right place, you don't think,

"Now I must extend my leg." Your leg extends automatically. Much of a newborn baby's movement is reflexive, and these reflexes are somewhat protective. There are around seventy primitive reflexes in the newborn period. I will describe only some of the most common and interesting reflexes, especially those that have survival benefits.

Sucking and swallowing is the most important survival reflex. Babies automatically suck in response to stimulation of (in decreasing levels of sensitivity) the soft palate, the interior of the mouth and lips, and the cheek and chin. These reflexes are most easily elicited close to baby's feeding time.

Tied in with the suck reflex is the **rooting or search reflex.** When mother's nipple tickles baby's face he will search or root for the nipple by turning his head and mouth. This reflex helps baby find the nipple more easily. I believe that the rooting reflex is important to nighttime nursing; the baby sleeps nestled up against mother's breasts and his reflexes help him zero in on the nipple and help himself to a nighttime feeding. (In our family we call this nighttime feeding "self-serve," as opposed to the "full serve" of the usual daytime nursing.)

These reflexes, also called mouthing reflexes, enable babies to find the source of food. A practical tip for breastfeeding: don't tickle baby's cheek to encourage him to latch on; this causes him to turn his head out of alignment, which may interfere with normal sucking and swallowing. It is better to turn the whole baby on his side to face your breasts, his tummy to your tummy, and stimulate your baby to open his mouth by brushing his lips with your nipple.

The **Moro reflex** occurs in response to a sudden, disturbing noise or a sudden withdrawal of support to a baby's head and back. In reaction to this sensation of falling, baby quickly extends his arms out from his body as if trying to cling to and embrace

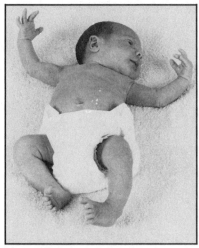

Moro reflex

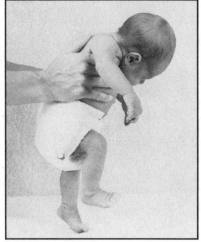

Stepping reflex

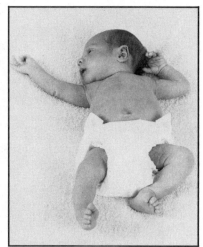

Tonic neck reflex

someone. This reflex is accompanied by grimacing or crying, especially if there is no one to grab on to for comfort. This clinging response is a protective reflex, and baby needs a person between those embracing little arms. This reflex gradually lessens and disappears by three or four months.

The **grasp reflex** is another protective reflex. It allows the baby to hold an object with his hands. If you stimulate the palm of your baby's hand with your finger (place your finger into the palm from the side of the hand opposite the thumb) his fingers will wrap tenaciously around yours. If you begin to lift your baby by your finger you will notice that his arm and wrist muscles tense as if helping to pull himself up. His grasp intensifies and has such strength that you can actually lift him partially off the surface he's lying on before he lets go (see photo). A similar reflex can be elicited by gently stroking the sole of your baby's feet behind the toes; his toes will grab your finger. The grasp reflex usually disappears by the third month. Anthropologists have speculated that the Moro reflex and the grasp reflex are remnants of attachment behaviors used by human infants to hold onto their mothers like other primates do.

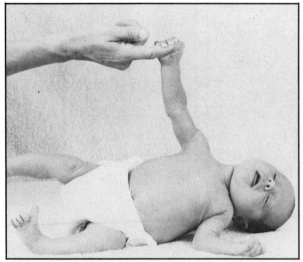

Grasp reflex

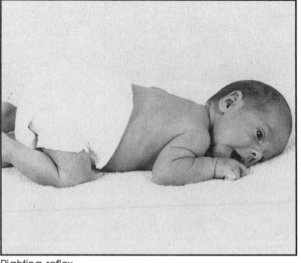

Righting reflex

The **withdrawal reflex** is often noticed in newborns during a blood test. If painful stimulus is given to the foot of the baby (such as pricking the heel to obtain blood) the leg and foot flex and withdraw to avoid the pain. At the same time, the other leg thrusts outward as if to push the painful stimulus away.

The **stepping reflex** is interesting and fun to test in your newborn. Hold your baby upright over a table so that the sole of one foot presses on the table. The weight-bearing foot will lift up and the other foot will lower as if the baby is beginning to take a step (see photo). This reflex usually disappears in the second month.

The Fencer's reflex (tonic neck reflex). If you turn a baby's head to one side while he is lying on his back, his arm and leg on that side will thrust outward while the opposite arm and leg flex, resembling the *en garde* position of a fencer (see photo). This reflex encourages baby to look at the hand extended in front of his face. In some ways it inhibits him from using his arms, hands, and head in midline play—in front of his body. The tonic neck reflex subsides around three to four months, allowing the infant to engage in stimulating hand-eye play.

Righting reflexes help baby learn to keep his head, trunk, arms, and legs in proper alignment for survival and motor development. They mature during the first year of life. The most obvious righting reflex in the newborn period is baby's attempt to keep his head where it ought to be in relation to the rest of his body. If you place your baby face down, he will momentarily lift his head just enough to clear the surface and turn it to one side (see photo). If you pull your baby up by his hands to a sitting position, he will tense and elevate his shoulders in an attempt to keep his large head from wobbling from side to side or overshooting the mark and falling forward.

Another interesting protective reflex might be called the **smothering avoidance reflex**. If a light blanket is placed over baby's nose and mouth, he will mouth it initially and then twist his head vigorously from side to side or cross each arm over his face in an attempt to knock the blanket off.

One reflex which begins in the newborn period and persists throughout life is the **gag reflex**. Stimulation of the back of the throat causes the jaw to lower and the tongue to thrust forward and downward. This automatically expels an object from baby's throat thus protecting him from choking while he learns to feed and swallow.

Your baby's reflexes are more than just curiosities. They are necessary to survival and development. Watching for them enhances your appreciation of this little person's amazing capabilities.

Your Newborn's Smiles

For years parents and professionals have debated the subject of just how early babies smile. Is it really a smile or is it just gas? After twenty years of watching our own six children and thousands of

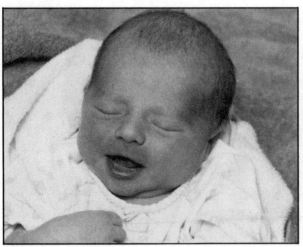

Sleep grin

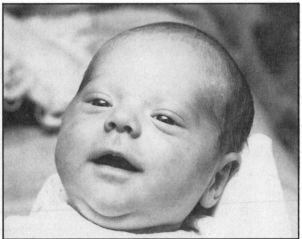

Early smile (three weeks)

other newborns, I have concluded that newborns truly do smile, even on the first day. I divide baby's smiles into two types: inside smiles and outside smiles. In the first few weeks, baby's smiles are a beautiful reflection of an inner feeling of rightness. These smiles usually occur while drifting off to sleep and are called sleep grins. Sleep grins come in many forms. Some are one-sided, some two-sided, some last for several seconds, some only a fleeting moment—a happy twitch in the corner of the mouth. Inside smiles are often accompanied by other signs of relaxation: baby goes totally limp and his arms dangle at his side, seemingly weightless. (I call this the "limp limb sign.") Newborns will often smile immediately after the release of tension. Another good time to catch a smile is right after they burp or pass gas. Baby's early smiles convey an "I feel good inside" message. Occasionally during the first month some outside stimulus such as your own smiling or facial expression may produce a smile on your baby's face. This outside, or social smiling, usually does not begin to any great degree until the second month. These smiles, when they appear, are a powerful reinforcer of caregiver activity.

"One of Matthew's (age one week) behaviors that has me totally entranced is his smile. When he smiles it seems to arise from a feeling of goodness and rightness deep down inside of him and when I see that smile I feel ecstatic, I feel so good. I feel the same sense of goodness and rightness start to spring up from inside my very soul and I feel so much at one with Matthew especially at this time. It's almost as though we are sharing a secret that neither one of us really knows the words to but we know the feelings to."

Opening Moves

Babies move a lot at all ages. Developing an appreciation for how your newborn uses his whole body sharpens your observation skills and will help you notice the subtle changes from month to month. When quiet or sleeping, newborn babies resume the fetal position, the position they grew accustomed to *in utero*: when lying on their tummies their legs are flexed up toward their abdomens and their feet are curled underneath the diaper area. Their bottoms are higher off the mattress than their heads. They can lift their heads and turn them just enough to make their noses clear the surface so they can breathe. Even as newborns, babies occasionally thrust out their legs as if trying to push off. When a newborn baby lies on his back, all his limbs are drawn in toward his body. His feet usually cross or touch each other.

You will notice that your newborn holds his hands close to his face most of the time. Periodically he rests his open hands on his face as if to stroke it; this is probably reminiscent of his actions *in utero*. Baby's fists are clenched, except when he is very relaxed or sleeping, a time when his fingers will relax a bit and his hands open.

When playing with your newborn you will notice that his muscles have a spring-like feel. When you pull his arms or legs away from his body or try to open his hands they quickly spring back to their original flexed position. As the weeks go by you will notice baby's muscle tone increasingly relax.

Baby's movements vary dramatically when he is lying on his back in a state of quite alertness. He may rapidly thrust his arms and legs outward for no reason and then slowly return them to his torso. When startled he may flail his limbs about in a jerky rhythm. Even when sleeping and apparently not upset, a newborn occasionally twitches and startles. The jerkiness of movements is especially prevalent in premature infants. Newborn babies also move their arms and legs in smooth, rhythmic, freely cycling movements resembling the action of a slow-motion movie. If you place your hands over baby's knee and elbow joints you will often hear and feel clicking or crackling sounds. These are normal joint noises caused by the rubber-like ligaments and loose bones.

Here are some exercises you can do from time to time with your baby to get to know his moves and see how his muscles develop from month to month. By getting to know the limitations of your baby's trunk and head movements during the first month you will appreciate how rapidly he gains control during the following months.

1. Face-down suspension: Hold your baby firmly around his middle. You will notice that his arms, legs, and head dangle and droop toward the ground. Occasionally he will flex his arms and legs toward his torso and attempt to raise his heavy head, but you can tell that he does not yet have the strength to overcome the force of gravity. Your newborn is somewhat aware of his position; as you lower him down toward the table or floor, notice that he rotates his head to one side (usually the right) to rest his cheek on the surface.

2. Sitting position: Hold your baby by his torso in the sitting position. You'll notice that his back is rounded and his head slumps forward onto his chest. As a newborn his muscles aren't strong enough to control his head, shoulders, or back.

3. Pull to sit: If you pull your baby by the hands from the lying to the sitting position you will notice that his head is wobbly and lags behind his shoulders. When his torso reaches a sitting position, his head overshoots the mark

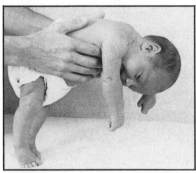

Ventral (face-down) suspension

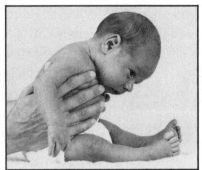

Early supported sitting

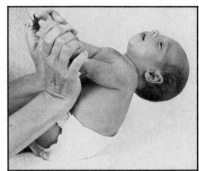

Pull to sit (note head lag)

and falls forward. You may notice that your baby's head and limb muscles seem stronger during the first week than toward the end of the first month. This is because in the first days after birth your baby's neck and limb muscles are still under the tightening effect of early reflexes. These reflexes diminish toward the end of the first month.

What Your Newborn Can See

Within a few hours after birth your newborn's eyes become less sensitive to the brightness of the world he has just entered, but he may continue to squint during sudden light changes such as going into bright sunlight. During their first few days babies' eyes are closed most of the time. This can be very frustrating for parents. Here is a little eye-opening trick which I use during newborn examinations: hold your baby in front of you with one hand supporting his head and the other under his bottom, approximately twelve inches from your eyes. Turning from the waist swing him gently through an arc of about 120 degrees and come to a slightly abrupt stop. This rotating motion prompts baby to open his eyes reflexively. Another method is to support your baby's head and bottom and raise him gently from a lying to a sitting position.

A newborn's visual acuity is estimated to be 300/20, which means that a newborn sees clearly only at 20 feet what an adult with normal vision can see clearly at 300 feet. Recent experiments have shown that the newborn can see much better than previously thought. Newborn babies focus best at a distance of eight to twelve inches, which corresponds to the usual eye-to-eye distance during breastfeeding.

Newborns like to look at the human face, the real thing or drawings or photos. Next in order of preference are black and white contrasting patterns—checkerboards, stripes (at least a half inch wide), and bull's-eyes—followed by medium intensity colors rather than bright reds and oranges.

TRACKING

Some newborns can follow an interesting object or person with their eyes from side to side for nearly 180 degrees. This is called tracking. If the object moves too fast or is more than twelve inches away they quickly lose interest. Because the tonic neck reflex keeps their heads turned toward the side, most newborns will follow moving objects for only ninety degrees, from side to center, before losing interest and turning away. Your newborn's eyes and head movements do not work together well. If you turn your baby's head, his eyes will follow slowly. If his eyes follow your face, his head rotation is somewhat jerky, as if the head is trying to catch up. Synchronous head and eye rotation does not occur until around age one month.

FIXATION

You will notice that your newborn's eyes often wander independently—he looks cross-eyed. While experiments have shown that newborns have the capability to coordinate both eyes momentarily, they usually can't do it all the time. Because they do not use both eyes together, the images do not fall on the same part of the retina in each eye. This results in poor depth perception. As babies learn to hold their heads and eyes still and coordinate their eye movement, images become clearer and depth perception improves. This is called binocular vision. It starts to develop around six weeks and is well-established by four months.

Tips to hold baby's visual attention

• Baby is in the quiet alert state.

• Keep object or face within twelve inches of baby's face

• Use large facial gestures (wide open mouth and eyes) while speaking in a slow, rhythmic, exaggerated fashion.

You may notice that your newborn's eyes occasionally fixate on yours, though only for a fleeting second or two. If you hold your face within baby's focal distance (twelve inches) when he is in the state of quiet alertness, he may look steadily at your eyes for five to ten seconds. During the first few weeks, when baby's eyes search and scan but are seldom still, parents will often plead with the baby to "look at me." Baby finally does look at you a bit longer around two weeks of age, and this often coincides with the beginning of smiling in reaction to someone else's gesture. Even though babies begin to be able to focus around two weeks, their eyes will continue to move independently most of the time. They also continue to lag behind the head when it is rotated side to side, a phenomenon called "doll's eyes." This response disappears by two or three months. A noticeable increase in staring and enlargement of the pupil size are other visual changes which occur around two weeks of age.

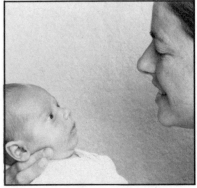
Brief eye contact at three weeks

The newborn baby has a limited ability to protect his eyes. He will blink in response to a startling noise or flash of light but will not blink protectively when an object is moving toward his eyes. This ability develops sometime during the second month.

Quiet alert

Active alert

Crying

Behavior states of infants

Quiet alert. Bright, open, attentive eyes. Limbs relatively quiet. Appears to be contemplating the environment. State most receptive to learning.

Active alert. Similar to quiet alert, but limbs and head are moving. Less visually attentive. Baby seems distracted by his own movement.

Crying. Loud, fretful complaints. Flailing, uncoordinated limb movements. Only minimally attentive. Behavior is upsetting to baby and to his caregivers.

Drowsiness. Eyes open and fluttering, slightly attentive. Quiet, stirring body movements. Baby is either waking up or falling asleep.

Sleep. In REM (rapid eye movement) sleep, there are spurts of movement, facial and limb twitches, irregular breathing. In non-REM sleep, there is minimal movement, regular breathing, and a calm, expressionless face.

HABITUATION

Newborns become bored easily by unchanging visual stimuli. They lose interest in a static figure such as concentric circles, horizontal stripes, or a picture of a face. A constantly changing figure, such as a human face with its changing expressions, retains baby's interest longer. In fact, the human face has a unique attraction for human infants. Researchers have shown that newborns pay the most attention to images which have the characteristics of the human face: contrasting light and dark areas, almost constant motion, constantly changing patterns, roundness, responsiveness to the infant's actions. The newborn is programmed to pay attention to the human face even from birth (Goren 1975). Researchers showed four different diagrams to forty

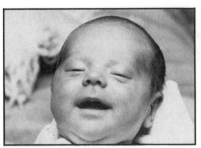
Drowsy

REM sleep

Non-REM (deep) sleep

newborns at a mean age of nine minutes. The babies turned their heads and eyes in a greater arc (sometimes approaching 180 degrees) towards the diagram which showed the facial parts in the right configuration. They showed less interest in diagrams in which the facial parts were scrambled. Many researchers feel that the responsiveness of newborns to the human face is inborn. As early as two weeks of age, a baby will watch his mother's face longer than that of a stranger (Carpenter 1974).

During the first month, newborns tend to be scanners. They tend to look more at the edges of the face than at the central features. During the second and third month the newborn is much more interested in the eyes, nose, and mouth—the features at the center of the face. The eye itself has qualities that appeal to newborns: shininess, light and dark contrasts. Babies also are fascinated by small moving objects—like the eye. Similarly mother's breasts are round and have contrasting light and dark areas which may naturally appeal to babies. Studies have shown that patterns stimulate sucking in the newborn. Perhaps this is why newborn babies suck better while looking at their mothers' faces. (Older babies may be distracted by visual stimuli and stop sucking.)

How widely a baby's eyes are open gives a clue to his state of relaxation and receptivity. Eyes that are slightly closed indicate that baby is drifting off and losing interest in his environment, especially when accompanied by relaxed and dangling arms with open hands. Closed but fluttering eyelids often mean that baby is in the state of **active sleep** (also called REM sleep, the time when adults dream). Closed non-mobile eyes and an expressionless face may mean that the baby is in a state of **deep sleep**. The face and especially the eyes can tell you a lot about what is going on in the baby's mind.

What Your Newborn Can Hear

Your newborn baby probably hears as well as an adult, but there are some things to note about newborn hearing. Newborn babies are more sensitive to loud and startling sounds; they may blink, jerk, or draw in their breath sharply. You will notice that your baby reacts differently to different sounds. While he may startle or shudder at loud, sharp noises, soft crooning noises produce fleeting smiles. Newborns prefer higher pitched voices. They are often soothed more easily by mother's high-pitched voice than by father's lower voice. Babies also are selective in their musical tastes. They calm when they hear classical music that has a regular rhythm and gentle dynamics. Music that has rapid volume changes or is just plain too loud (like rock and roll) may make them startle or just tune out. Newborns have a remarkable capability for protecting themselves from unpleasant noises. They can selectively block out disturbing noises. This is called the stimulus barrier. Because of it, you may find it difficult to test your baby's hearing. Sometimes babies simply will not react to a loud noise and at other times they will. Early in the newborn period, the stimulus barrier is more pronounced. Toward the end of the first month they seem to react more to a noisy environment.

Mothers often are confused about whether or not their babies hear them. The baby may not turn his head toward the sound of your voice for two or three months. Also, babies who are with their mothers constantly may become habituated to their mothers' voices; a baby hears his mother's voice so often that he stops reacting every time she speaks. However, studies have shown that the newborn baby can distinguish his own mother's voice from that of a stranger (Miles 1974). When researchers placed babies twenty to thirty days old behind a screen so that they could hear the voices but not see the speaker, the babies sucked faster and longer in response to their own mothers' voices as compared to those of strangers.

Newborn babies soon learn that mother's voice comes from her mouth. In one study, a mother spoke to her baby through a glass screen. The baby could see the mother through the glass but could hear her only by means of two stereo speakers, one on each side of the baby. The balance between the speakers could be adjusted so that the sound appeared to come from straight ahead or from the sides. The babies in the study were content when the sound appeared to come from straight ahead, i.e., from the mother's mouth, but they were disturbed if the sound came from another direction (Bower 1974).

Cognitive Development

During the early weeks of life, the infant learns to fit into the caregiving environment. To help establish the fit, the newborn comes programmed with qualities called attachment-promoting behaviors. These automatic behaviors get the parent-infant care system rolling. Throughout his development, the infant refines these attachment-promoting behaviors in order to cement and strengthen the bond with his parents. The most noticeable attachment-promoting behavior is the infant's cry.

The newborn's cries are undifferentiated. The cry may mean hunger, cold, or distress. A newborn seldom has different cries for different needs, nor does the parent perceive any differences from one cry to another. These early newborn cries are largely automatic reflexes. The baby does not think, "I'm hungry, so I must cry to get fed." How, then, are these reflexes translated into cognitive behaviors in which the infant thinks before he acts?

Most of a newborn's learning is directed toward the goals of comfort and satisfaction. For example, a newborn must learn how to suck efficiently in order to gain the reward of more milk. A baby also learns that his distress signals will result in a response: "If I cry, I will be picked up and fed." With continued repetition of the cue-response pattern, the infant develops a mental model of the whole exchange. Researchers refer to this mental pattern as a schema. So, although the initial behavior of the infant is reflexive rather than cognitive, the repetition of the sequence (distress is followed by comfort) enables the infant to learn a cognitive behavior and to store the pattern in his mind. Eventually, when he is picked up, he will be able to anticipate that a feeding will follow and will orient himself toward the breast. The more sensitive and responsive the caregiver is to the cues of the infant, the better these early reflexive behaviors translate into thought-out behaviors.

Any discussion of cognitive development must take into account the response of the caregiving environment to the signals of the infant. Early researchers in infant development did not fully appreciate this fact. In reality the parent and the baby develop together, each affecting the other's responses. Baby's initial stimulus is reflexive (distress generates crying), and mother's is cognitive ("Should I pick the baby up and nurse him?"). As the pair practices this cue-response behavior the baby's actions become more cognitive ("If I cry, Mommy will come and nurse me"), and the mother's responses become more intuitive.

HOW YOUR BABY LEARNS TO TALK

Even as early as one day of age your newborn may move in synchrony with your voice and speaking gestures. This early body language is the beginning of your baby's speech. During the first month, you may not consciously notice any reaction from your baby when speaking to him, but he does react even though it may be imperceptible to your eyes. Researchers who analyzed films frame by frame noted that the listening baby seemed to dance in time to the rhythm of mother's voice (Condon 1974). As the mother spoke, the infant made slight but constant movements of the head, eyes, shoulders, arms, hands, and feet. Remarkably, these movements started, stopped, or changed in almost perfect synchrony with mother's speech. Further analysis of these high-speed films showed that infants are highly sensitive to differences in sounds within the same word. For example, babies showed three distinct responses to the three basic sounds (phonemes) in "over"—the o, the v, and the er. Because your baby's reaction to your speech during the first month is so subtle, you do not usually realize that you are getting through to your baby.

Mothers instinctively use upbeat tones and facial gestures to talk to babies. They E-X-A-G-G-E-R-A-T-E. The sing-song quality of mother's speech is tailored to the baby's listening abilities. Mothers speed up and slow down. Vowel duration is longer ("goood baaaby"). Mothers talk in slowly rising crescendos and decrescendos with bursts and pauses, allowing a baby some time to process each short vocal package before the next communication arrives. How a mother talks to her baby is more important than what she says.

Analysis of mother-baby communication has shown that what seems to be a monologue by the mother is actually an imaginary dialogue. Although the infant rarely vocalizes back, the mother generally behaves as if he had. She naturally shortens her messages and elongates her pauses; the length of the pauses coincides with the length of the imagined response from the infant, especially when she is talking to the baby in the form of questions. In this early "taking turns" type of speech, mother is shaping the infant's responses. He will store this information away and use it later when he becomes truly verbal.

In the first month, mother-baby talk is more for bonding than for exchange of information. Do make an effort to talk to your baby, even if you feel self-conscious at first. Talk to him about what you're doing or tell him all about himself. As visual and attentive capabilities increase over the next several months, mothers and babies begin taking turns, and they also vocalize in unison, called **chorusing**. Chorusing is more likely to occur when interaction during speech becomes more lively and engaging.

Get used to addressing your baby by name. "Hi, Matthew!" If you use your baby's name frequently, he will soon recognize it. You will engage his attention more quickly and hold it longer if you open your dialogue with his name and repeat it frequently during the conversation. While he does not yet associate the name with himself, hearing it frequently triggers associations with the special sound he has heard before. He perks up and pays attention, much like adults do when they hear a familiar tune.

Getting to know your baby during the first month is an exciting, interesting, and sometimes exhausting process. Discovering his capabilities right from the start will make your parenting job easier and more enjoyable in the months—and years—to come.

SUMMARY: *BIRTH TO ONE MONTH*

	Large motor

• Lifts and rotates head to clear surface when lying on tummy.

• Limbs flexed as *in utero*. Asymmetric posture predominates when lying on back.

• Head lags behind, overshoots, and droops forward when pulled to sitting position. Head drops forward when held sitting.

• Bears no weight on legs, exhibits stepping reflex.

Fine motor

• Hands in tight fists; clenches rattle when inserted into hand, but drops it immediately.

• Looks at but does not reach for toy in front of him; can follow moving object ninety degrees from side to center.

Language/ social

• Crying is undifferentiated and demanding; no anticipatory pauses.

• Moves in synchrony with mother's voice.

• Throaty, grunting sounds.

• Exhibits inborn attachment-promoting behaviors.

Cognitive

• Learns to suck efficiently; orients to breast in anticipation of nursing.

• Internal smiles, sleep grins

• Scans periphery of parent's face; may fixate on eyes for a few seconds; prefers to look at faces, light and dark contrasts.

• Distinguishes mother's voice from stranger.

CHAPTER FOUR:

Feeding Your Baby

Proper nutrition or the lack of it can have a profound effect on your baby's growth and development. Good feeding techniques—the art of feeding—can also have a profound effect on your role as parents since during the first year you will spend more time feeding your baby than in any other parent-baby interaction. When you choose to breastfeed your baby you are guaranteeing him the best nourishment and the best nurturing. You are tapping into a formula for mothering and feeding as old as time itself, tested, and true.

Breastfeeding

Breastfeeding is a lifestyle, not just a method of feeding. When you realize how breastfeeding benefits mother, baby and family, you will be more determined to overcome any difficulties that may arise in the early days or weeks of your breastfeeding experience. Because breastfeeding is the next step in the continuum of pregnancy and childbirth, there are physiologic advantages to the mother. The closeness required by breastfeeding, combined with the mothering cues from prolactin, practically guarantee the initiation of the bonding process. Add to these primary advantages the fact that your milk is always at the right temperature, fresh, clean, and instantly available and you have the best and easiest feeding system there is, at the lowest possible cost.

The advantages of breastfeeding for baby are even more impressive. Your milk, like your blood, is a living substance. It is custom-made, beginning with colostrum, the special substance in your breasts during pregnancy and in the first few days after birth before the milk comes in. Colostrum provides heavy doses of immunity from disease. It is a protein-rich food, and a natural laxative which clears the meconium from baby's intestines. Human milk contains special proteins designed to promote brain growth, the most important organ of our species. All the elements are there in just the right proportion—fats, sugars, proteins, minerals (including iron), vitamins, and enzymes. Even the way your baby sucks at your breast is important. The special action required during breastfeeding enhances the development of baby's oral muscles and facial bones. The emotional advantages to mother and baby are overwhelming. Studies have shown that skin-to-skin contact and touching benefit baby's physical and emotional development.

HOW BREASTFEEDING WORKS

The lactation system inside your breast resembles a tree: the glandular tissues are the leaves where the milk is produced, the ducts are the branches where the milk moves down into what would be the trunk of the tree, the milk sinuses, which are reservoirs in which the milk collects waiting to be released into baby's mouth through the nipple. These milk sinuses are located behind your areola (the dark area surrounding your nipple). Milk empties from the sinuses through approximately twenty openings in your nipple. To effectively empty these milk sinuses, your baby's gums must be positioned *over* them so that his jaws compress the sinuses where the milk is pooled. If baby sucks only on your nipple, little milk will be drawn out and your nipple will be irritated unnecessarily. Baby should have at least one inch of your areola in his mouth.

When your baby sucks, the nerve endings in your nipple stimulate the pituitary gland in your brain to secrete prolactin. This prolactin stimulates your milk glands to produce more milk. The first milk your baby receives at each feeding is the foremilk, which is thin because of its low fat content. As your baby continues sucking, the nerve endings stimulate the pituitary gland to secrete another hormone called oxytocin. This hormone causes the tissue around your milk glands to contract like a rubber band and squeeze a large supply of milk from the milk glands into the sinuses. This later milk, or hindmilk, is much higher in fat and slightly higher in protein and therefore has greater nutritional value. The hindmilk is the primary nutrient for your infant's growth.

Most mothers have a tingling sensation in their breasts as the hindmilk is let down from the milk glands into the milk sinuses. This is called the let-down reflex or milk-ejection reflex. A successful milk-ejection reflex is a key to successful breastfeeding. This reflex is characterized by a feeling of fullness or tingling which occurs about thirty to sixty seconds after baby has started suckling and may occur several times during a feeding. Mothers feel this milk-ejection reflex in different intensities at different times. Most first-time mothers will begin to notice this reflex by the second or third week after beginning breastfeeding. Some mothers never feel it, but may recognize it by the leaking that occurs. Your milk-releasing hormones can be inhibited by fear, tension, pain and fatigue.

Milk production works on the supply and demand principle: the more your infant sucks, the more milk you will produce, until you have both negotiated a proper balance. Your baby develops a "timer" for his feedings, and your breasts and pituitary are synchronized to your baby's timer. For example, a mother may feel a milk-ejection reflex (her timer) at the same time her baby cries for a feeding, although the two may be miles apart. Breastfeeding problems occur when this timer and the supply and demand relationship are upset.

How your infant sucks. Aroused by the touch of your nipple to his lips and the scent of your milk, your infant's lips grasp the areola of your breast and his tongue draws your nipple into and against the roof of his mouth. Your infant's lips and gums compress the areola and underlying milk sinuses, pushing milk toward the nipple. The infant's lips and the large fat pads in the cheeks provide an effective seal, creating negative pressure in the mouth. The infant's tongue then milks the areola in a rhythmic motion, drawing the nipple toward the back of the tongue, and pressing out the little squirts of milk which are then swallowed. Sucking milk from a bottle through a rubber nipple is a very different process. Because milk flows more easily from a bottle, nipple and jaw compression and negative pressure are less necessary and the milking action of the tongue is different. The difference between sucking actions required on breast and bottle nipples may lead to **nipple confusion** if baby is given bottles during the first few weeks when he is learning proper sucking.

GETTING STARTED BREASTFEEDING

Breastfeed immediately after birth. Unless a medical condition prevents it, your first breastfeeding can occur just minutes after your baby's birth. Both mother and baby benefit from being together immediately after birth. This is the time when baby will be in a state of quiet alertness and very receptive towards sucking. After his initial cries are soothed he will gaze around, searching for your face and eyes and reaching out with his mouth for your breast. Guide his movement and let him nuzzle your nipple, licking and making his attempts to suck. This first sucking at the breast is baby's first lesson in breastfeeding, given at a time of optimal receptivity to learning how to suck, and it sets the stage for subsequent learning.

Position yourself and your baby properly. Sitting up in a bed or rocking chair is your easiest position for nursing. Pillows are a real must. Place them behind your back, on your lap to hold your baby, and under the elbow that will support your baby's head. Get comfortable before beginning to nurse.

Undress your baby in front to promote skin-to-skin contact. Nestle baby in your arm so that his neck rests in the bend of your elbow, his back along your forearm, and his buttocks in your hand. Turn baby's entire body so he is facing you, tummy to tummy. His head should be straight, not arched backward or turned sideways in relation to the rest of his body. Your baby should not have to turn his head or strain his neck to reach your nipple. (Turn your head to the side or up to the ceiling and try to swallow!) Baby must also be up at the level of your breasts, so you will need a pillow or two on your

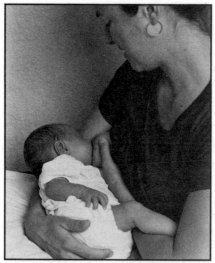
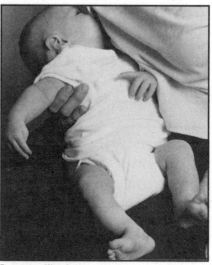

Proper positioning in the cradle hold   Poor positioning

lap. It helps to raise your lap more by putting your feet on a footstool. If you try to hold baby up with your arms, your back and arm muscles will be strained. If baby rests low on your lap, he will be pulling down on your breast causing unnecessary stretching and friction. As you turn baby on his side, tuck his lower arm into the soft pocket between him and your midriff, bending him so he is wrapped around you. This basic position is called the **cradle hold** (see photos).

Encourage proper latch-on. With your free hand, manually express a few drops of milk to moisten your nipple. Cup your breast, supporting the weight of your breast with your fingers underneath and your thumb on top, your hand back toward your chest wall to keep it clear of the areola. If you have large breasts, you might want to use a rolled hand towel under your breast to support the weight so that it doesn't drag down on baby's jaw and tire him out.

Gently tickle your baby's lips with your milk-moistened nipple, encouraging baby to open his mouth *wide*. Babies' mouths open like little birds' beaks—very wide—and then quickly close. The moment your baby opens his mouth wide, direct your nipple into his mouth (be sure to place it above his tongue) and with a rapid movement, pull him *very close* to you with the arm that is holding him. This technique is known as **R.A.M. (Rapid Arm Movement)**. Don't lean forward, pushing your breast toward your baby. Pull him toward you. Most new mothers do not pull their babies close enough.

Attempt to get a large part of your areola into his mouth. Maximize the amount of areola in his mouth by flanging his lips outward; do not allow him to tighten his lips inward. The key to correct latch-on is for your baby to suck on the areola, the dark area of your breast surrounding your nipple. Pull your baby so close that the tip of his nose touches your breast. Don't be afraid of blocking his nose, since he can breathe quite well from the sides of his nose even if the tip is compressed. If baby's nose does seem to be blocked, use your thumb to press gently on your breast to uncover his nose.

If you have flat or inverted nipples or a baby with a weak suck, there is an additional step you need to use. As soon as baby has latched on and starts to suck, compress your breast by pressing in with your thumb and fingers—this stabilizes the milk ducts and holds them forward so baby does not lose his grasp so easily.

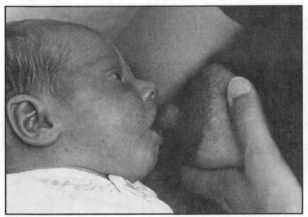

Tickling baby's lips encourages him to open wide.

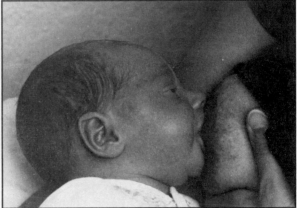

Latched on

As you R.A.M. baby on, be sure that your nipple is centered in his mouth and that baby does not slide onto the nipple. His gums should completely bypass the nipple and come to rest about an inch behind the nipple on the areola. If you do it quickly enough, his mouth will close down far back on your areola, not on the nubbin of your nipple. If your baby is latching-on correctly, you should not feel painful pressure on your nipple. Remember, babies should suck the areola, not the nipple. If baby seems to be sucking incorrectly, you may have to make him stop sucking (break the suction with your finger between his lips and gums) and start over several times until you get it right. Don't allow your baby to continue wrong sucking; it hurts you and is incorrect patterning and a habit that is hard to break. Some babies learn to slide onto the nipple, slurping it in as they go but stopping short of the ideal position. This results in a frustrated baby who gets little milk and a mother with sore nipples. If baby persistently clamps down too hard, tell him to "open" while depressing his lower jaw with your finger on his chin. You should notice instant relief from the pain. If your baby does not cooperate, break the suction and start again. It is important that he learns to suck the right way. Many babies suck correctly as a natural instinct, but some babies have to be taught.

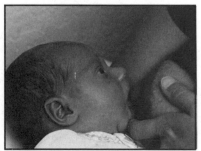

Depressing the lower jaw with the index finger

Babies exhibit various sucking styles. Some babies latch right on and suck like pros the minute they find the nipple, while other babies seem more interested in looking around or lazily playing with the nipple. Slow starters who like to suck a little and snooze a little need some prodding and need to sleep skin-to-skin in their mothers' arms. With constant encouragement, the sleepy baby gradually will suck longer and more enthusiastically. After a few weeks you will notice that your baby exhibits two types of sucking: comfort sucking, a weaker suck primarily with the lips in which your baby gets the foremilk; and nutritional sucking, a more vigorous sucking with the tongue and jaw. You will notice the muscles of his face working so hard that even his ears wiggle during intense nutritional sucking. This kind of productive sucking rewards your baby with the higher-calorie hindmilk. The visible contractions of your baby's jaw muscles and the audible swallow sounds are reliable indications that your baby has good sucking techniques.

Alternative nursing positions. Two other basic breastfeeding positions you need to know are the **clutch hold** and the **lying down position**. By varying the way you hold baby to feed him, you will be less likely to get sore nipples because baby's mouth will be putting pressure on different points on the areola and nipple. For both these positions the method of getting baby to latch on is the same as for the cradle hold. If you have had a cesarean birth, it may be easier for you to nurse your baby lying down (see photo). The lying down position is basically the cradle hold but with baby and mother lying on their sides facing each other. Place pillows under your head, behind your back, under your top leg, and a fourth pillow tucked behind baby so your arm doesn't have to continue to hold baby close to you once you drift off to sleep. Place your baby on his side facing you, nestled in your arm, and slide him up or down so his mouth lines up with your nipple. Use the same positioning and latch-on techniques as described for the cradle hold.

Another nursing arrangement for a cesarean mother or a baby who has difficulty latching-on is the "clutch hold" (see photo). Position baby under your arm along the same side as the breast you are using. Place a pillow at your side and put your baby on the pillow. Cup the back of his neck in your hand and bend his legs upward so that they are resting against the pillow supporting your back.

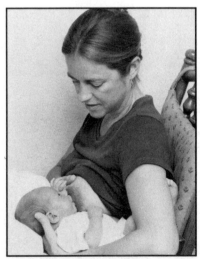

Clutch hold

Pull baby in close to you (R.A.M.), and once baby is sucking well push a pillow or two against his back to hold him close. Lean back in your bed or chair and enjoy the feeding. Be sure baby is not pushing with his feet against the back of the chair or pillow, causing him to arch his body. If this happens bend baby at his hips with his legs and buttocks up against the chair back. The clutch hold is especially effective for babies who squirm, arch their backs, and frequently detach themselves from the breast.

COMMON BREASTFEEDING QUESTIONS

"How often and how long should I feed my baby?" Early in your breastfeeding relationship you will realize that the term schedule has absolutely no meaning to a baby. The only schedule your baby will have, and should have, is his own. Breastfeeding is more than a mathematical exercise. One nursing mother put it this way, "I don't count the number of feedings any more than I count the number of kisses." One of the most beautiful and natural biological negotiations is a mother and her suckling baby working together to get their own biological clocks synchronized and the law of supply and demand working comfortably. Listen to your baby's cues and watch your baby, not the clock. Remember, it is the *frequency* of nursing, more than the duration of each feeding, that stimulates your milk-producing hormones.

In the first few days most babies suckle in varying intensities, intermittently, and for long periods of time, even as long as an hour. Baby will often fall asleep during a feeding and then wake up in an hour and want to feed again. The duration of the feeding often depends upon baby's sucking styles. Little gourmets suck gently and intermittently while playing with the nipple and looking around, whereas "barracudas" get down to business quickly and feed ravenously. If your baby is latching-on correctly your nipples will not get sore from nursing frequently and long. Learn to read your baby for signs of hunger and contentment instead of watching the clock. Breastfeeding cannot be scheduled easily because babies digest breast milk more rapidly than formula; therefore, breastfed babies feel hungry more often and need to be fed more often. Babies have growth spurts during which they need more food for more growth. Babies also enjoy periods of nonnutritive sucking in which they are more interested in the feel than in the food. Sometimes babies are only thirsty and suck a little to obtain some of the watery foremilk. Expect your baby to breastfeed every two to three hours around the clock (or ten to twelve times a day) for the first month or two. In the first few days don't be discouraged if your breastfeeding relationship does not go as smoothly as you hope. It takes some nursing pairs a while to get used to each other. Let your baby fall asleep at your breast. Just being close to your baby and letting his mouth touch your breast will stimulate your milk to come in.

"Does my baby need any bottles?" Unless advised otherwise for a medical reason, breastfeeding babies do not need supplemental bottles of formula or water. Sucking on artifical nipples may lead to nipple confusion and throw mother and baby out of synchrony. Bottles of water are not necessary when babies have physiologic jaundice.

"What if my nipples are getting sore?" Teaching your baby to latch-on correctly to your areola is the best preventive medicine for sore nipples. At the first sign of nipple soreness, scrutinize your technique of positioning and latch-on to be sure you are not letting baby apply most of the pressure to your nipples rather than to your areola. Be sure your nipples are completely dry when not "in use." Use fresh nursing pads, without plastic liners, to be sure no moisture is in contact with your tender skin. Let your nipples dry thoroughly before you put your bra flaps up. If you're in a hurry, try using a blow-dryer to speed this process. A pure oil to which neither mother or father are allergic, completely massaged into the nipples after nursing, can provide local soothing and healing. The best ointment for sore nipples is colostrum or breast milk. Do not use oils or creams that need to be washed off before nursing. The little bumps on your areola around your nipple are glands that secrete a cleansing and lubricating oil to protect the nipples and keep them clean. Avoid using soap on your nipples since it may encourage dryness and cracking and removes these natural cleansing and lubricating oils. Careful sunbathing (only for a few minutes) can also speed healing.

If your nipples are getting sore from baby clamping down too hard, review the steps for positioning and latch-on. Pull down baby's lower jaw slightly during sucking, and pull him closer into your breast during nursing. Nurse baby on the side that is least sore first, and encourage more frequent, shorter feeds. If baby needs to be pacified and your nipples are wearing out, let him suck on an index finger instead of a pacifier in the early weeks to avoid nipple confusion or poor suck patterns. Cut your nail short and get the finger in as far as you can, about one and a half inches. If nipple soreness continues, consult your La Leche League Leader.

"What if I don't have enough milk?" Most delays in milk production are the result of improper positioning and latch-on or interference in the harmony between mother and baby. Giving supplemental bottles, mother-baby separation, and scheduled feedings are the common causes of delayed lactation.

Checklist for a good milk supply

1. Avoid supplemental bottles unless medically necessary.

2. Temporarily shelve all other commitments that drain your energy away from your baby.

3. Avoid negative advisers. ("Are you sure he's getting enough?") Surround yourself with supportive people.

4. Take your baby to bed with you and nurse nestled close to each other.

5. Increase the frequency of feedings to at least one feeding every two hours. Wake your baby if he sleeps more than three hours.

6. While you are nursing, look at, caress, and groom your baby. These maternal behaviors stimulate the milk-producing hormones.

7. Sleep while your baby sleeps. This requires delaying or delegating many of the seemingly pressing household chores. If you are blessed with a baby who nurses frequently, you may think, "I don't get anything done." But you are getting something done. You are doing the most important job in the world—mothering a human being.

8. Undress your baby during nursing for more skin-to-skin contact. If baby is small, under eight pounds, you need to keep him warm with a blanket around him, still allowing tummy-to-tummy skin contact.

9. Try **switch nursing**. Switch nursing, also called the "burp-and-switch technique," operates as follows. Let your baby nurse on the first breast until the intensity of his suck and swallow diminishes and his eyes start to close (usually three to five minutes). Remove him from this breast and burp him well; then, switch to the next breast until his sucking diminishes again, stop, burp him a second time and repeat the entire process. This helps baby get more of the creamier, high-calorie hindmilk and is particularly effective for the sleepy baby who does not nurse very enthusiastically.

10. Try double nursing. After you nurse your baby and he seems to be content, carry him around in a baby carrier instead of immediately putting him down to sleep. Burp him well and about ten to twenty minutes following a feeding nurse him again. This allows the trapped bubble of air to be burped up, leaving room for a topping-off.

11. Be sure you are able to relax during feeding. The milk ejection reflex can be inhibited if you are tense physically or emotionally. Use the relaxation techniques you learned in childbirth class, use pillows, have someone rub your back, visualize flowing streams, feel confident in yourself.

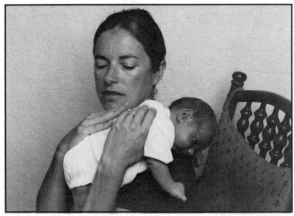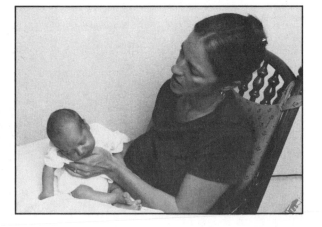

Burping techniques

12. Get support from breastfeeding and mothering organizations such as La Leche League. This network of breastfeeding mothers can provide you with the support you will need during those confusing first few months. Breastfeeding is a confidence game. A good support group will help you to develop this confidence.

13. If you are still having a problem, don't give up. Contact a La Leche League Leader for more help.

"How do I know that my baby is getting enough milk?" After the first month or two you will know intuitively that your baby is getting enough milk. He will feel and look heavier. In the first few weeks it is not as easy to tell that your baby is getting enough milk, especially if you are a first-time mother.

Signs that your baby is getting enough milk

1. In the early weeks your baby will have wet diapers often, at least six to eight wet cloth diapers (four to five paper diapers) and two or more bowel movements per day.

2. Your breasts may feel full before feedings and less full after feedings, and leak between feedings.

3. If you feel your baby sucking vigorously, hear him swallowing, feel your milk-ejection reflex, and then see your baby drift contentedly off to sleep, chances are he has gotten enough milk.

"What happens if I have too much milk (become engorged)?" If you are rooming-in and feeding your baby as needed, your milk will come in sooner, within twenty-four to forty-eight hours, but gradually, so that you will have less engorgement (a sudden filling and swelling of the breasts causing them to be very hard and painful and difficult for the baby to get a good latch-on). Engorgement is your body's signal that the supply and demand is out of balance. If engorgement occurs in the hospital, use an electric breast pump to release some of the extra milk in order to soften the areola so that baby can latch on better and more effectively empty your breast. At home, engorgement can be dealt with by learning a good manual expression technique. (The Marmet Technique pamphlet listed in the suggested readings is available through La Leche League.) A warm shower or warm soaking in a basin or warm compresses before expressing will help your milk ejection reflex so you can let go of some of this overabundance. Encouraging baby to suck frequently and effectively is the best way to prevent continued engorgement.

Do not let this engorgement become increasingly painful since continued engorgement can lead to a breast infection. If a breast infection (mastitis) occurs, above all, *don't stop nursing!* The breast must be emptied. Immersing your engorged breasts in comfortably hot water for ten minutes can facilitate emptying. Use ice packs between feedings to alleviate any discomfort. If your breast is so hard that the milk cannot flow, use continuous covered ice packs to reduce the internal swelling. If high fever, chills, fatigue, and increasing soreness and redness of your breasts occur, then you may need antibiotics. Call your doctor if you have these symptoms. Your baby can still breastfeed while you are taking antibiotics.

Drink extra water and rest as much as possible. Call La Leche League for more information.

Engorgement in the later weeks is often due to an upset in the baby's or family's routine—too many visitors, missed feedings, too many outside activities, excessive use of supplemental formulas, anything that throws the "timer" out of balance.

"Why does my baby want to nurse all the time?"
In the first few months babies have **frequency days** when all they want to do is nurse. This is called "marathon nursing." The supply-and-demand principle of breastfeeding is working in response to baby's sudden growth spurts. Your baby may also be going through a period of high need. Some babies want and need to be held and nursed all the time during the first few months as they slowly adjust to life outside the womb.

"What should my diet be during breastfeeding?"
Basically you should maintain the well-balanced high protein diet that you had during your pregnancy. Avoid junk foods which are high in calories and low in nutrition. Some mothers wish to hasten their return to their pre-pregnancy weight. Avoid crash diets as they are not healthy for either a nursing mother or the baby. Exercise is the safest way for the lactating mother to control her weight. Drink at least eight glasses of water a day.

"What foods should I avoid while breastfeeding?"
Some foods may upset some babies. Caffeine-containing foods such as colas, chocolate, and coffee, if taken in excess, may upset the baby. Some babies may also be allergic to dairy products in their mothers' diet. You can usually enjoy a normal diet during breastfeeding.

"How can my husband help in breastfeeding?"
Many fathers feel left out of the inner circle of the breastfeeding pair but fathers do, in fact, play an extremely important role in the successful breast-

feeding relationship. In surveys of those factors which contribute to successful breastfeeding, a sensitive and supportive father was high on the list. To encourage father involvement, it used to be advised that fathers give an occasional bottle to the baby. We do not advise this custom because of the possible interference in the law of supply and demand, the harmony and synchrony which occur between mother and baby. What works better and is more biologically sound is for the father to indirectly feed baby by improving the care and feeding of the mother. One father in a successful breastfeeding family summed it up very wisely, "I can't breastfeed our baby, but I can create an environment which helps my wife breastfeed better." Fathers can bathe, walk, play, and help with baby. Breastfeeding is indeed a family affair.

Formula Feeding

There are mothers for whom breastfeeding does not work out or who may choose to feed their babies with infant formula. Whether you are breastfeeding or bottle-feeding, the time you spend feeding your baby is important. "Nursing" should mean comforting and nourishing—whether by breast or bottle. Here are some suggestions on how you and your baby can enjoy bottle-feeding.

Touch your baby. Feeding your baby is not just delivering milk. Feedings also deliver emotional nourishment. Your baby should always feel that a person is feeding him, not just a bottle. Therefore it is not a good idea to prop bottles. Hold your baby while you feed him, and hold the bottle as though it were coming from your body. Many mothers have enjoyed bottle-feeding more when they maximize the amount of skin-to-skin contact they have with their babies during feedings.

Eye contact. Look into your baby's eyes when he looks up at you during feedings. You and your baby may both have a tendency to let your attention wander during bottle-feedings. Looking at your baby's beautiful face and body will help you keep your attention focused on him.

Interact with your baby during pauses in the feeding. Babies usually feed in short bursts of sucking interspersed with restful pauses. Most babies, breastfed and bottle-fed, feed better if you are quiet while they suck, but they often enjoy social interaction during the pauses. Watch your baby for the times when he is ready for some feeding conversations. Eventually you will develop an intuitive sense of your baby's feeding rhythms.

Cue-feeding. Learn to read your baby's cues in order to differentiate hunger, thirst, and distress. Whether you are breastfeeding or bottle-feeding, your response should be to pick up the baby and respond to his need. The breastfeeding mother offers the breast, and baby can suck according to what he·needs, whether for food or comfort. Bottle-feeding mothers have to figure out what the specific need is and offer the appropriate response. It is not always necessary to offer formula—occasionally, you can offer a bottle of water to a formula-fed baby. (Bottle-fed babies should receive extra water because formula is too concentrated for immature kidneys.) And, of course, baby will need other kinds of nurturing and interaction at times when he is not hungry.

How much, how often, what kind? Generally in the first six months when your baby is growing rapidly, he should receive two to two-and-a-half ounces of formula per day per pound of body weight (or 125-150 ml/kg/day). In other words, if your baby weighs ten pounds, he should take twenty to twenty-five ounces (560-700 ml) of formula daily. From six to twelve months, the daily volume of formula either remains the same or gradually diminishes as your baby's intake of solid food increases. Commercial infant formulas are available in three basic forms: powdered, liquid concentrate, and ready-to-feed. Which form you choose is largely a matter of economics and convenience. Follow the directions on the container carefully when preparing formula and add the specified amount of water—no more, no less. Ask your physician for advice on what kind of formula to use.

Tiny babies have tiny tummies. Smaller, more frequent feedings are best. Because formula is not as quickly digested as breast milk, formula-fed babies may go longer between feedings, and it may be easier to schedule feedings. Cue-feeding is equally important for bottle-feeding mothers. Even if you schedule feedings every three hours, you will want to be flexible if baby is hungry sooner or sleeps a little longer. And baby will still need lots of non-scheduled, non-feeding nurturing time in response to his cues.

Starting Solids

The eagerness for early introduction of solids has lessened in recent years for a variety of reasons. Most mothers now breastfeed and breastfeed longer. Commercial formulas and baby foods have been improved, and research on infant nutrition has shed new light on the when and why of introducing solid foods.

Breast milk or commercial formula or a combination of the two contains all the essential nutrients your baby needs for the first four to six months. Parents often offer solids much earlier than the baby needs or wants them. Prior to six months your baby doesn't need solid foods for nutritional reasons, but developmentally he may be ready for them at four or five months. If your baby watches your food go from your plate to your mouth or if he reaches for food from your plate he is showing signs of readiness.

Try this to see how your baby reacts to solid food: use your finger to place a small amount of mashed, very ripe banana on the tip of your baby's tongue. If his tongue goes in and he smiles with approval, baby is ready; if the banana comes right back out, accompanied by a disapproving grimace, baby is probably not ready. A baby's tongue is carefully designed to protect the intestines from too much food too soon. Early on, babies have a tongue-thrusting reflex, meaning the tongue will protrude outward when any foreign substance is placed upon it. This protects babies against choking on solid foods or other things placed in the mouth. Around four to six months this tongue-thrust reflex diminishes, another indication that solids should be delayed until that time.

The rest of baby's digestive tract is not designed for early solids either. The intestines are not equipped to handle a variety of foods until around four to six months when a number of digestive enzymes

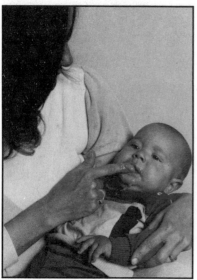
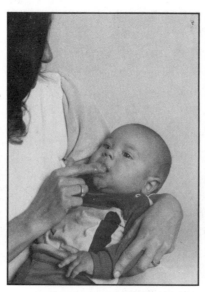
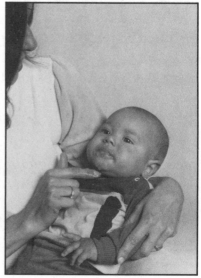

First taste of mashed ripe banana

appear in significant amounts. Pediatric allergists in particular discourage the early introduction of solids. In the first few months baby's immature intestines may allow potential allergens to seep into the blood stream, increasing the risk of the child developing food allergies. As the intestines mature they become like filters which screen out the larger, potentially allergenic protein molecules or digest them into smaller, less allergenic substances. Teeth seldom appear until six or seven months—further evidence that the young infant is primarily designed to suck, not chew.

FIRST FOODS

Start with solid foods which are close to milk in taste and consistency, for example, mashed bananas. Remember, baby has to develop an entirely new mechanism for eating, changing from sucking to swallowing to tongue-mashing and swallowing. Around six months babies develop two skills which make feeding much easier: the ability to sit up in a high chair and the ability to pick up small objects.

Besides using your fingers or a spoon to feed baby, you can also allow him to feed himself and capitalize on his rapidly developing hand skills. Place a glob of mashed banana within grabbing distance on his table or highchair tray. Six-month-old babies pounce on anything of interest placed in front of them. You will notice that your baby will soon be able to pick up a morsel of food between thumb and fingers and gradually find his mouth with it. In the beginning stages there may be more misses than hits, and much of the food gets splattered over baby's cheeks. Sharing the food with his face and shirt is part of the game. Allow your baby the experience of trial and error; practice eventually makes perfect. Remember that an activity initiated by baby has more learning value and holds his attention longer than one initiated by the parent.

Besides mashed bananas, cereals are a favorite early food. Rice and barley are the least likely to cause allergies. Mix the cereal with expressed breast milk or formula, and gradually change to a stiffer and lumpier consistency when your baby shows chewing actions and is able to guide the solids with his tongue. Do not put cereal in a bottle with formula. It is confusing to a baby to get solids through a nipple, which he has learned is for sucking. Gradually introducing foods of thicker consistency encourages baby to learn chewing and swallowing skills. There are a variety of spoons and infant dishes (besides your fingers and baby's hands) available to help with the feeding experience. Expect your baby to treat solids as toys. He will watch the food splash on the floor and enjoy your reaction to this nutritious little mess. Here's a tip for getting most of the food where it belongs, a maneuver I call "the upper lip sweep." Place the finger or spoonful of solids in baby's mouth and allow his upper lip to sweep the food off as you gently lift upward and outward with the spoon.

TABLE TALK

Talk to your baby during feeding. Talk about both the food and the procedure so that he learns to relate the words to the type of food and the interaction that is soon to follow: "Matthew want banana? Open mouth!" Open your own mouth in hopes that baby will mimic your facial gestures. Talking to your baby about feeding also helps you know if baby is truly interested in eating at a certain time. If your baby's face lights up and his mouth opens as you talk about the feeding, this is a clue that he is receptive. Talking about an interaction that is soon to follow is called a **setting event**; the words and gestures set up the familiar interaction that will follow. Setting events teach baby to anticipate what will happen and allow him to communicate his desires.

Observe stop signs. Pursed lips, a closed mouth, the head turning away are all signals that baby does not want the food on the spoon. Don't force-feed, especially in the early months. Babies under four months seldom accept solids cheerfully, and many may need gentle encouragement even around six months. Others show no interest even as late as eight or nine months. You want your baby to develop a healthy attitude both toward the food and the feeding.

One of the common myths about feeding solid foods is the idea that if you fill baby up with cereal he will sleep through the night. As a tired father of six, I, too, have considered this temptation. However, controlled studies have shown that infants who are fed solids before bedtime do not sleep any better than infants who are not.

It is wise to introduce new foods at least one week apart, in case a baby may prove to be intolerant or allergic to a certain food. The usual signs of food allergy include bloating and gasiness, a sandpaper-like rash on the face, a runny nose and watery eyes, diarrhea, waking at night, and generally cranky behavior. The following are favorite starter foods: bananas, rice and barley cereals, applesauce, peaches, pears, carrots, squash, sweet potatoes, mashed potatoes, and avocados.

How much at a time. Start with about one teaspoon of each new food. Your initial goal is to introduce your baby to new tastes and new textures, not to fill him up. Vary the texture and the amount to suit the mouth skills of your baby. Some babies like a thinner consistency and large amounts; others do better with thicker foods and smaller amounts.

I have noticed that breastfed babies are less eager to accept solid foods, and breastfeeding mothers are less enthusiastic about offering them. Perhaps this is because of the uniquely satisfying experience that breastfeeding is for babies and mothers. During the first year, consider solids an addition to, not a substitute for, milk, especially if you are breastfeeding. Your baby *needs* milk; he may *want* solids.

Offer solids at a time of the day when baby seems hungry, bored, or you both need a change of pace. Choose a time that is convenient for you since a little mess is an inevitable part of the feeding game. For many babies late afternoon is a favorite time. This seems especially true for breastfed babies. Mornings are usually the best time for offering solids to formula-fed infants because then you have the most time with your infant and usually do not have to worry about preparing a meal for the rest of the family. A breastfed infant should be offered solids when your milk supply is lowest, usually toward the end of the day. Since infants have no concepts of breakfast, lunch, and dinner, it really makes no different what they receive when.

Reading the feeding cues of your baby, encouraging self-feeding, and advancing gradually all help to create a healthy feeding attitude. To a baby eating is not only a nutritional necessity but also a developmental skill. The more a baby enjoys an experience the more efficiently he will advance in using those skills. Infant feeding not only provides fun and nutrition for baby; it also helps parents observe and enjoy their baby's rapidly developing hand skills. By now you may have caught on to a very important point about feeding your infant: feeding is a social interaction, not just a nutritional exercise. There is a person at *both* ends of the feeding, whether it be by breast, bottle, or spoon.

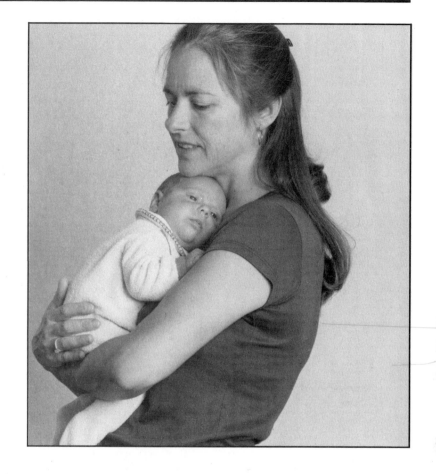

Finally Connected

"I finally feel connected to him," explained my wife, Martha, overjoyed by the exciting changes in our six-week-old Matthew. During the second month you will begin to feel that you are really getting through to your baby. The first month you put in; the second month you get back. Your growing baby will seem more responsive, more expressive. He seems to open up. Eyes are open wider. He is more alert. His hands open up and the fingers extend. He smiles. This is his social debut; he is coming out of himself.

During the first month your newborn was getting organized. Most of his energy was spent adjusting to life after birth. He was trying to fit into his new family, he was discovering to whom he belongs, he was learning to trust. He was developing a feeling of rightness during the first month, and this feeling makes it possible for his personality to begin unfolding. The energy that was previously spent getting organized can now be used to interact with his environment. Feelings are translated into action in the second month.

Visual Development

The eyes of the two-month-old are open wider and can focus longer and follow objects better. While the one-month-old can see clearly only within one to two feet, the two-month-old can focus on things that are eight to ten feet away. His world is widening. Because he sees persons and objects more clearly, he enjoys his world more and stares at it longer. You will notice your baby studying your face, mesmerized by what he sees. The fleeting glances of the first month evolve into five to ten seconds of engaging eye-to-eye contact that absolutely captivates caregivers. Your baby's eyes seem to say "Hi, Mom! Hi, Dad!"

The visual scanning which was characteristic of the first month now begins to take in more detail. Watch your baby study your face at a distance of twelve to fifteen inches. Baby first scans the periphery, paying attention to the general outline and contour. He then zeros in on the central details: eyes, nose, mouth. His interest goes where the action is, to your moving eyes and mouth.

Imitation. Your baby's interest in moving faces leads to the development of another skill: imitation. Your baby attempts to mimic your changing facial expressions. This visual imitation game may become like

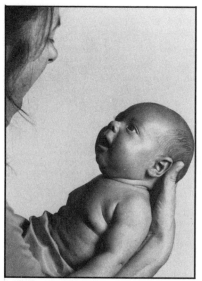

Imitating mother's expression (nine weeks)

dancing—you lead, and baby follows. Your baby's ability to imitate you reinforces your feelings that you really are getting through to this little person with big eyes. Reinforce your baby's interest in this game by responding to what he's doing: talk to him, exaggerate your facial expressions, imitate him. By taking your turn in this exchange, you extend baby's interest in this dialogue.

During the second month, baby's eye movements become smoother. His eyes and head begin to move together. Toward the end of the second month he may be able to track a slowly moving object or face from side to side for a full 180 degrees. He now pays attention to faces or dangled objects held to the side. His eyes will follow you for a few moments as you walk away.

Visual accommodation. In the first month baby had little interest in the world beyond his reach because that was as far as he could see clearly. In the second month, he becomes able to focus on objects at greater distances. This refined focusing ability, which has effects similar to changing lenses in a camera, is called visual accommodation. Baby's focus goes from wide-angle to telephoto, pausing momentarily as if to snap the pictures he likes. Visual accommodation is most noticeable when you hold your baby in front of you at a distance of one to two feet. Baby will study your face a while, then gradually shift his gaze to focus on an interesting object eight to ten feet away, and then again shift back to peer at your face.

Studying mother's face

"When Matthew is looking at me, he scans my face very methodically and systematically. He seems to be studying my face. He will start out looking at my eyes and from there he will look up to my hairline and follow the hairline all the way around, then come back to the eyes, down to the mouth, up to the hairline and back to the eyes. He will study my face like this for long periods of time."

Babies' eyes are the window to their feelings and state of alertness. Wide-open "sparkly" eyes are invitations to interaction. Slowly closing or droopy eyelids signal that sleep is coming. When your baby turns away from eye-to-eye contact, he is telling you that he's losing interest and it's time for a change. His moving eyebrows add even more expressions to his visual language.

Here's a way to tell how far your baby sees clearly. Engage your baby in eye-to-eye contact from a few feet away. Slowly move backwards, increasing the distance between you and the baby, while you keep making faces that will hold his attention. Your baby will lose interest and break the eye contact when you are out of focus. You can also tell how far your baby can see by figuring out what he's looking at. When his eyes fix for five to ten seconds on some object across the room or on the ceiling (babies like the light and dark contrast of a beamed ceiling), you know that your baby can see objects at that distance.

What one-to-two-month-old babies like to look at

Contrasts and contours. Black and white designs are still the favorite.

Large glossy **black-and-white photos** of mom's and dad's faces.

Broad stripes, approximately two inches wide.

Black dots, one inch in diameter, on a white background. (The younger the baby, the wider the stripes and the larger the black dots and blocks.)

Checkerboards and bull's-eyes. The two-month old is more interested in circular patterns than in stripes.

Mobiles, especially ones that feature the black-and-white contrasting designs listed above.

Themselves in **mirrors.**

Ceiling fans.

Fires in fireplaces.

Ceiling beams.

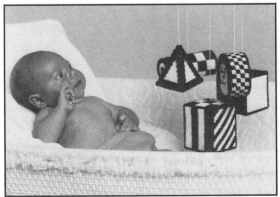

Alert and interested

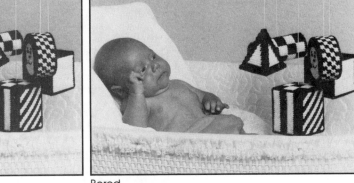

Bored

While pastel colors are favored by decorators for babies' rooms, they are the least favorite of babies. During the first few months, babies like black and white better than a rainbow of colors. They prefer colors that contrast each other rather than soft colors that blend together. Even at this age, human beings prefer the colors of nature over synthetics. Flowers in the garden, the reds and yellows of changing autumn leaves, or even bare tree branches against a winter sky may be more interesting to babies than pastel designer wallpaper. If you want to stimulate your baby's visual sense, take him outside. The rhythmical movement of trees, clouds, waves, and flowers will fascinate him.

Babies' eyes are still a bit sensitive to light at two months so you may notice that he is more visually attentive in dimmer lights than in bright lights, which may cause him to squint and slowly blink. Babies are also more visually attentive when upright. When babies lie on their backs, they seem to be less interested in using their visual or motor skills to relate to their environment. Perhaps the reclining position reminds them too much of sleep. Instead of letting your baby lie on his back in a crib gazing at dangling mobiles, sit him upright in an infant seat or on your lap, or carry him over your shoulder, and you will notice that he spends more time looking around at faces and objects.

TIPS FOR VISUAL STIMULATION

Eye color often deepens during the second month, giving a clue to what your baby's permanent eye color will be. Some babies' eyes do not arrive at their permanent color until six months.

How Your Two-Month-Old Moves

Between one and two months your baby's movements begin to mature. They are less controlled by reflexes than they were in the early weeks. Over the next several months your baby will discover his body—what it looks like and all the things it can do.

HAND AND ARM MOVEMENTS

During the second month, baby notices his hands. Now that he can see more clearly, he begins to use his most accessible tools—his hands. He wants to swipe at what he sees. A familiar principle of motor development states that intent precedes ability. This is certainly true of reaching. Babies' first attempts to reach out may be more like little punches, short little jabs in the direction of the desired object or person. At first you may regard these cute little jabs as aimless arm movements, but if you watch closely you will notice some directionality in these early reaches. Baby seems to punch in the direction he is looking. If you look over the ends of his fists you will often see the eyes staring in the direction of his reach. While reaching ability varies from baby to baby, most two-month-olds have a low hit rate. Their hands seldom strike their intended target. Babies also take great delight in sucking on their newly discovered fingers.

During the second month, babies' limbs relax a bit. Instead of always flexing their arms and legs inward, toward their bodies, they open up and stretch out. Their fingers are no longer clenched into fists. Instead, when babies are in the alert state, the thumb and then the fingers begin, one by one,

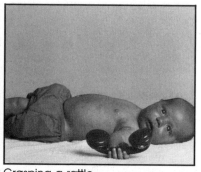
Grasping a rattle

to fan out, another early sign of intended reaching. Most two-month-olds do not voluntarily grasp at dangled objects, but they can hold a toy or a rattle briefly if it is placed securely in their little hands. When your baby's fists are clenched, stroking the back of his hand may stimulate him to open up and loosen his grip.

Most babies show a preference for the right side, turning more often to the right than to the left. (This is not predictive of whether the baby will be right- or left-handed in the future.) This preference usually diminishes by the third month.

LEGS AND TORSO MOVEMENT

Your two-month-old will also relax his leg muscles. Instead of drawing up his legs, frog-like, toward his body, he spends a lot of time with his legs extended. When lying on their stomachs, babies this age may stretch out fully. If their extended legs happen to come in contact with a surface, they may unexpectedly push off and propel themselves forward. When lying on their backs, babies like to bicycle with their legs, one of the earliest motor activites that uses both sides of their bodies. A two-month-old baby can bear some of his weight on his legs for at least a few seconds before they give out. This early practice at standing is reinforced when baby is held face to face against a parent's familiar body; he can then "stand" on the parent's supporting hands or lap (see photo).

Rolling over. The two-month-old has more muscle strength and greater control. His head, arm, and leg movements are less jerky, the result of a maturing nervous system. The increased maturity of leg and arm movements makes it possible for babies to roll. I have found that the timing and sequence of rolling over varies greatly among babies. Most two-month-old babies can roll ninety degrees—from back to side or side to back. Occasionally when a baby is

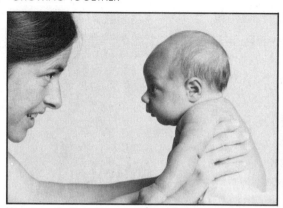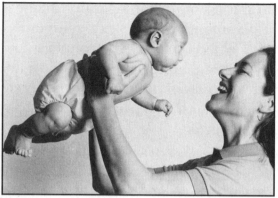

Head control and muscle strength improve in the second month.

lying on his stomach he may tuck one arm and shoulder underneath himself and push up with the other arm so forcefully that he rolls from front to back, surprising himself (and his parents) with his success.

Head control improves remarkably during the second month. When pulled by the hands to the supported sitting position, babies' heads still lag behind and bob around when upright, but their heads are much less likely to overshoot the mark and fall forward. Two-month-olds can hold their heads erect and turn them toward each shoulder for a few seconds before their neck muscles succumb to the front head droop. When lying face down, they are able to raise their heads at a forty-five degree angle for a few seconds, more often looking to one side than straight ahead. If you get down to meet his eyes, baby may sustain his head lift longer, looking straight at you.

You can see your baby's overall improvement in muscle control by holding him up in the air by his hips and torso. (This is called **ventral suspension**.) You will notice that his arms and legs are less droopy than they were as a newborn and that he holds his head in line with his trunk. His arms, though, are still drawn in toward his body. Babies usually don't "fly" with their arms and legs straight out until the next month.

Two-Month Talk

During the second month babies' throaty, grunting sounds become higher pitched, more vowel-like, and more pleasant and musical. Their repertoire of sounds includes coos, squeaks, gurgles, and mews. Toward the end of the second month babies' increased saliva production may give these early sounds a sputtering quality, a prelude to the bubble-blowing that starts a few months later.

Babies' vocalizations range from brief one-syllable squeaks and squeals to prolonged, almost two-syllable, expressive sounds consisting of a single vowel: "ah, eh, oh!" Sounds made during sleep amuse and sometimes worry parents. Babies' breathing may sound rattled as the air moves through the saliva-filled throat. You may notice momentary cooing sounds while your baby is sleeping—as if he is dreaming.

During the second month the sounds your baby makes give you a clue as to what mood he is in. Cooing sounds are babies' earliest attempts to communicate delight. Remember that language is made up of both sound and gesture. For example, notice the amusing sounds that accompany a smile. The initial part of the smile (the mouth opening) is often accompanied by a brief "ah" or "ugh," followed quickly by a long sighing, cooing sound as the smile widens and grows.

TIPS FOR CONVERSING WITH YOUR BABY

Look at and visually engage your baby before talking to him. While some babies begin to locate and turn toward the sound source at this age, others are disturbed when they don't see the person who is talking to them. When you make sure that your baby is looking at you before you initiate a conversation, you will be able to hold his attention longer. You are also more likely to get a response.

Babies respond to animated conversation.

Use short, two or three word sentences and one- or two-syllable words. Babies like lively exclamations or interchanges that end with question marks: "Hi, Matthew! Pretty baby! Where's Mommy?" Elongate the vowels: "B-a-a-a-by!" Pause frequently to allow baby to process and respond to your language. Notice your baby's limbs, eyes, and mouth while you speak and when you pause. His eyes are watching you; his limbs are moving in harmony with your gestures or they may slow down when you speak. These signs indicate that your baby is learning all the patterns that go into language—sounds, pitch, pauses, and gestures.

Be responsive. At every developmental stage, responsiveness is the key to language development. In the early months your baby cries and gives you cues in gestures and sounds—"pick me up" signs or "feed me" cues. Respond to him; this motivates him to "talk" better. Responsiveness teaches your two-month-old a valuable lesson: his cues warrant a response from his caregivers. This feeling helps him develop a sense of competency which, in turn, leads to self-esteem. This will be very important to him as he grows older.

Encourage happy sounds. By creating an environment which lessens the need for baby to cry in order to have his needs met, you make it possible for him to spend more time in the state of quiet alertness, a state that produces happy sounds. When babies need to cry less, they can learn to talk better.

Sounds babies like

Music boxes, musical mobiles

Classical music on the radio or stereo

"Sweet talk," for example, "What a happy baby!"

Soft talk. Softly saying "I love you" has a calming effect.

Singing, especially when dad croons low-pitched songs such as "Old Man River"

Household noises: running water, the dishwasher or

vacuum cleaner, etc. (Some babies don't like the noise of loud appliances.)

People talking

Ocean waves, waterfalls, streams

Sounds babies dislike

Sudden, loud, startling noises like doors slamming, hands clapping, yelling

Loud rock music

Household noises. Noises from such things as blenders or washing machines may startle supersensitive babies, yet calm others.

Social Behavior

Baby's smile. A baby's first smile makes his parents feel that all their efforts are worthwhile. The infant's smile develops through two stages. The newborn's smiles are reflex smiles, an automatic reaction to some inner feeling of rightness. They usually involve only the muscles of the mouth, and they often appear as a baby is drifting off to sleep. You may not even feel that they are real smiles.

During the second month these reflex smiles evolve into responsive smiles, smiles that are reactions to some outside stimulus, primarily a parent's smiling face. These smiles occur when baby is awake and alert, especially in the morning. They involve the whole face; sometimes baby's entire body wiggles with pleasure during a smiling game. Dimples appear in baby's chubby cheeks as he flashes his pearly gums in toothless grins. His eyes are wide open or, if he is really into it, crinkled up at the corners.

Responsive smile

A baby's smiles of contentment and pleasure are the beginning of language, the beginning of communication. You know how your baby feels by the way he smiles. There is a spirit of excitement in the smile of a two-month-old, as well as in those on the receiving end of that smile. Reinforce your baby's smiling by smiling back. Studies have shown that babies whose mothers smile at them frequently smile more themselves.

The two-month smile is a powerful reinforcer of parenting behavior. During the first month, babies use crying to tell you that they need someone to pick them up and spend time with them. So at least some of the time you spend with your baby is in self-defense. The smile, like the cry, is an attachment-promoting behavior, but it works in a different way. Smiling makes you want to interact with your baby. As babies mature, they use their smiles to influence parental behavior.

ENGAGING BEHAVIORS

During the second month babies develop social behaviors which let you know how they feel and where you stand with them. They learn to give cues that help you figure out how they feel about themselves and that indicate that they are developing trust in their care-giving worlds.

Anticipation and protest behaviors. By two months, babies whose parents have responded to the needs they express begin to manifest signs of trust. The earliest of these is anticipation. At this age babies discover that certain actions of theirs will elicit predictable reactions from care-givers. Babies learn to anticipate predictable sequences of needs, cues, and responses. When baby gives a cue that tells you about his needs, he anticipates that you will read his cue correctly and respond. He shows his anticipation by his excited behavior. If his cues are not read correctly or not responded to as quickly as he anticipates, he protests. Protesting is a survival behavior that helps to ensure that babies' needs are met. The "easy" babies who don't fuss can actually be more difficult to parent because it's harder to know what they need and they show less appreciation when you read their cues correctly. Anticipation and protest behaviors are most noticeable in relation to feeding.

"Matthew lets me know when he is hungry, and he knows that I usually hold him cradled in my arms for feeding. He knows that I fiddle with my blouse and unhook my bra to get ready, so already during this ritual he is letting me know that he is anticipating a feeding. He starts to nuzzle a bit, to change his breathing patterns, and to turn toward me in an expectant sort of way. He has already told me that he is hungry, and now he is telling me that he expects to be fed.

"If I miss Matthew's early cues, he proceeds to the next level. He pounds at my chest with his tiny little fists in a desperate kind of way and bobs his head back and forth. One day as I was preparing to feed him, I decided to hand him over to Dad so that I could get one more thing done before I actually sat down to feed Matthew. He immediately started to howl. This was the opposite of what he was expecting and wanting. He really was angry and got very upset and wouldn't settle down until I satisfied his anticipation and fed him.

"I have found it much more pleasant for both Matthew and me if I respect his anticipatory behaviors. When he has given me a cue that he is hungry and I respond immediately he is a wonderful sight. He looks at me with eyes that are anticipating the pleasure of being fed. His mouth starts to move and make smacking noises and his hands and arms are moving in a gathering-in sort of way. His whole body gets ready for the feeding, and as long as I don't take too long with getting ready, he continues in this anticipatory state and then nurses well. If I miss his hunger cues or try to delay a feeding, he may cry for a period of time and his mouth will be very tight and his lips pursed. During the feeding he will continue to be upset. His sucking movements will be tense and his face will be quivering. Disappointing his expectations produces feelings of mistrust which are reflected in his sucking patterns. Because of this, I find that my response time is getting shorter."

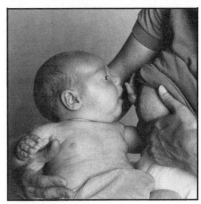

Anticipating a feeding

Mood sensitivity. Just as you are growing to know the needs of your baby, your baby is becoming sensitive to your moods. When mother is upset, baby is upset. I have noticed that the babies who are most sensitive to their parents' feelings are the ones who have a great deal of trust in their parents. This mutual sensitivity develops naturally when two people grow close to each other.

"We have observed through the past few weeks that our baby picks up our moods. When he was seven weeks old, the whole week I was very tired and depressed and unsettled. During that week he showed very little liveliness or responsiveness and didn't smile very much. He was just very blah. Then the next week, when I was feeling much better, the sparkle returned to our baby's personality."

FEEDING BEHAVIORS

By two months of age (if not much sooner) you will have realized that feeding schedules are an illusion, at least where breastfed babies are concerned. It is more important to think in terms of feeding harmony—getting to know your baby and his needs—than it is to try to get your baby on a schedule. Harmony means taking your cues from your baby rather from the clock. Harmony means that you feed your baby on cue (I prefer this to "on demand") rather than on a schedule.

The distracted nurser. A common feeding problem that occurs during the second month or later is the distracted nurser, "Mr. Suck-a-Little, Look-a-Little." Now that baby can see clearly for a distance of eight to ten feet, his interests widen. He looks beyond your face and body while nursing to his ever-widening world. He will suck a little, then stop and look at some interesting object or person, and then resume sucking. During the second month, some babies can master the art of doing two things at once, sucking while looking at other objects in the room. Being able to concentrate on two senses at the same time is an important ability which usually appears during the second month. But if being a distracted nurser is causing your baby not to nurse well or is making it uncomfortable for you (after all, your nipple will only stretch so far), nursing in a dark, quiet, uninteresting room ("sheltered nursing") for at least a few feedings a day will usually improve the situation.

"Be quiet and let me eat." Many babies do not suck as well if mother is talking during nursings. Some mothers try to encourage their babies to nurse by talking to them, but this may only distract some babies. Babies are better able to listen and suck simultaneously when they get older.

Medical Concerns

The two-month cough. A common health concern that appears during the second month is the two-month cough. At this age, babies begin producing a lot of saliva, often faster than they can swallow it. Saliva then collects in the back of the throat or goes down the wrong way, which stimulates a cough. This two-month cough is more a nuisance than a real medical problem, as long as baby seems generally well, and it usually disappears by the third or fourth month, when babies' swallowing ability improves.

All this saliva can produce a puddle of drool on baby's bedsheets, which in turn results in an irritating rash on the chin and cheeks where baby's sensitive skin has pressed against the saliva-soaked sheet. You will also notice your baby's increased saliva production when he is upright; his drooling gives him a wet shirt and you a wet shoulder. Babies have a knack for sharing their body fluids with their parents.

Safety tips. Because babies are more fun and responsive starting in the second month, older siblings often want to play with them. Teach your older children about what babies like and dislike and how to hold them safely and comfortably. Lay down rules such as the following:

1. You may pick up the baby only when mommy or daddy is in the room.

2. Always support baby's head. (Show how, and teach different ways of holding the baby.)

3. Move gently and slowly; don't shake the baby.

4. Speak softly; don't startle the baby.

5. Keep dangerous objects, such as sharp toys or tiny objects, away from the baby.

Help your older children to see that babies are very interesting. You might show them the pictures in this book to help them understand what their baby brother or sister can do now and what he or she will be able to do in the coming months.

Games for siblings to play with baby

1. Mommy's little helper—changing diapers (or handing them to you), helping with bathtime, deciding what baby should wear, etc.

2. Sing songs to the baby.

3. Hold the baby (with supervision).

4. Entertain baby when mommy is in the shower or making supper. (Siblings often excel at this.)

Finding Time to Relax

It is common for many babies, especially those with a strong attachment to their mothers, to not want to be put down or to be entertained by anyone other than their mothers. Some mothers even find it difficult to take a shower without loud protests. There are a number of ways to solve this problem. Try taking a shower with your baby. Some babies do like both the skin contact and the spray of the water. Or, play peek-a-boo with your baby from behind the shower curtain as he sits in an infant seat on the bathroom floor. If you're able to leave the shower curtain open, sometimes the sound of the water plus watching you will be enough to hold baby's attention, allowing you a few minutes of much-needed relaxation. Another alternative is to take a bath with your baby. This can be very relaxing for both mother and baby. You can nurse your baby in the bath, with only his head above water at the level of your breast. To get in and out of the bath safely with your baby, cover his infant seat with towels and place him in it. Then get into the bathtub yourself, sit down, and reach over and pick him up. When it's time to get out, place him in the seat, wrap him warmly in the towels, and you'll have a few minutes to finish getting clean on your own.

SUMMARY: *ONE TO TWO MONTHS*

Large motor

- Lifts head to forty-five degree angle when lying on tummy.
- Improving head control: can hold head erect momentarily when sitting, but head lags when pulled up to sitting position.
- Limbs are less flexed; legs extend, stretch out when lying on tummy.
- Legs and arms move more rhythmically.
- Rolls from back to side.

Fine motor

- Begins to relax fists, unfold fingers.
- Grasps and briefly holds toy placed in hand.
- Swipes at dangling toy; more misses than hits.

Language/social

- Higher pitched, happy sounds.
- Coos, squeals, gurgles.
- Produces vowel-like sounds: "ah," "eh," "oh."
- Smiles in response to others.
- Shows emotions: excitement, distress, delight, protest.
- Communicates needs; anticipates responses; cries when put down.

Cognitive

- Studies periphery of face; sustains eye-to-eye contact five to ten seconds during feedings; imitates facial gestures.
- Looks at and can follow movements of persons a few feet away.
- Can locate sounds, though not consistently.

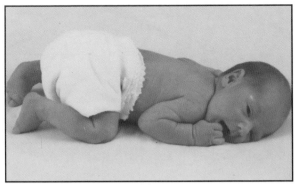
Lifting the head (one month)

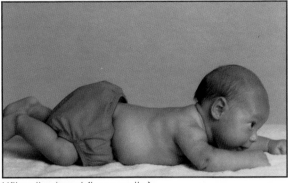
Lifting the head (two months)

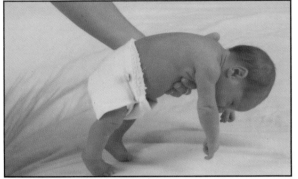
Ventral (face-down) suspension (one month)

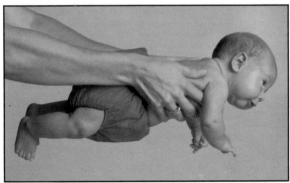
Ventral suspension (two months)

Pull to sit (one month)

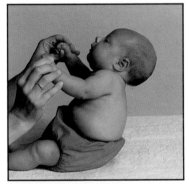
Pull to sit (two months)

GROSS MOTOR DEVELOPMENT

Babies' motor skills develop gradually month by month. Head control and neck strength improve greatly between the first and second month.

Sitting with support (one month)

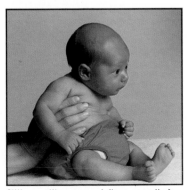
Sitting with support (two months)

Sitting supported (three months)

Balancing for a moment on one hand (four months)

LEARNING TO SIT ALONE

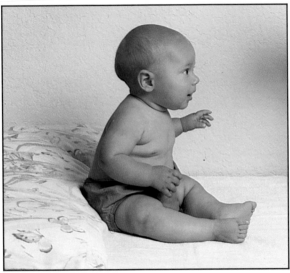

Sitting alone

Toppling over (five to six months)

Sitting and playing—the true test of sitting ability

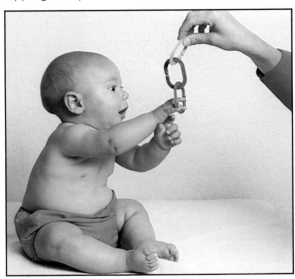

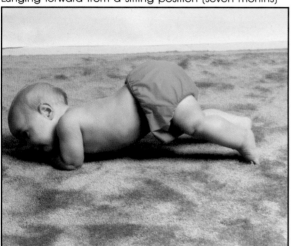

Lunging forward from a sitting position (seven months)

BEGINNING
TO CRAWL

"Commando" crawling (seven months)

Bridging on elbows and feet. One good push and forward he goes.

Going from sitting to crawling (nine months)

Cross crawling: opposite arms and legs move together (nine months).

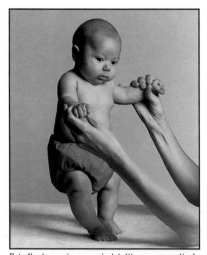

Briefly bearing weight (three months)

Scaling up furniture (eight months)

Standing with mother's help (five months)

Leaning against sofa (seven months)

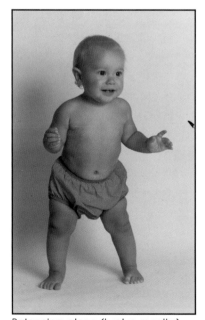

Balancing alone (twelve months)

First steps (twelve months)

STANDING, BALANCING, WALKING

CHAPTER SIX: THE THIRD MONTH

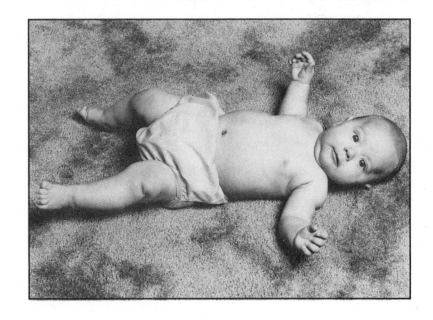

Baby Unfolds

The third month is a delightful period for both baby and parents. Baby is more alert, active, organized, and responsive. Communication is easier by the third month because parents and baby have become comfortable with each other's cues. In general, parents often describe the third month as easier.

During the first two months, babies' motor activity is influenced by newborn reflexes, which cause them to tighten their muscles and draw their limbs in towards their bodies. During the third month, their arm movements become more purposeful and begin to come under control of the higher brain centers. This enables them to use freestyle limb movements and hand-to-mouth activities to calm themselves down. Babies of this age seem to be putting more thought into what they do. They loosen up, and their bodies seem to unfold before your eyes.

Hand Play

The beginning of hand play is the most interesting feature of the third month, as babies discover that their hands are potential toys. They gradually unfold their closed fists, and their hands remain half-open most of the time. Sometimes baby's hands come together in front of his face and he looks at them and begins to explore and play with them. He may grasp one hand with the other, sometimes holding the whole fist, other times just one or two fingers. Baby's hands will often find their way to his favorite target, his mouth, resulting in the delight of fist and finger sucking. During this stage, babies realize that their hands are familiar, easily accessible, and most importantly, part of themselves.

If your baby is still tight-fisted at this age, try gently stroking the back of his hand. This stimulates a reflex which encourages baby to uncurl his fingers.

GRASPING AND REACHING SKILLS

If you place a ring or rattle into baby's half-open hand, his fingers will curl around it. Now, instead of dropping it immediately (as he did a few weeks ago), he will hold on and even glance at it momentarily until he drops it because he is tired or bored. The lighter the rattle and the easier it is to grip, the longer the baby will hold it. Babies usually prefer black-and-white fabric rattles at this age. Some babies will begin to show momentary interest in the sound of the rattle. This is the beginning of one of the most important kinds of play activities in infant development: contingency play. Baby's action (shaking the rattle) produces a reaction (the sound). Baby learns that the reaction is contingent upon his own voluntary action.

Babies practice their grasping skills on more than toys. Three-month-olds begin to grab at their par-

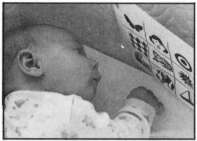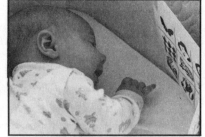

The beginning of accurate reaching

ents' clothing, mommy's blouse during nursing or daddy's tie while sitting on his lap. When you put your finger into the palm of baby's hand, notice how tightly he clenches it and how he tries to pull himself up while holding on. Baby takes great delight in grabbing mommy's hair or daddy's mustache or chest hair. He also enjoys your reaction.

Looking at your baby's eyes and hands will tell you when he is in the mood to play. If his eyes are wide open and looking at you and his hands are open with the fingers fanned out towards you, you will know that he wants to get his hands on some object or person.

The three-month-old also has more power behind those curious little hands. While most arm movements are still boxer-like karate chops, they gradually develop into a smoother, more calculated reach, however inconsistent and inaccurate. Sometimes baby may bat or swipe at a dangling mobile; other times he may swing out his arms to each side (flapping his "wings") or throw them around like a windmill until he slowly encircles the object, eventually getting it in his hands in a hugging movement. Tactually elicited grasping (baby grabs a toy when it touches his fingers) is more characteristic of this age than visually initiated reaching (baby reaches out and grasps an object dangled before his eyes), which develops later. For a dangling mobile to sustain the interest of a three-month-old, it must be in his line of vision and within touching distance.

Babies often lose interest in mobiles that are beyond their reach, no matter how interesting the design.

Safety tip

Always stay with your baby while you have a mobile within his reach. His fingers, or worse, his neck, can get caught in the dangling strings.

Hand play and hand-eye coordination in reaching is best stimulated by placing babies in a semi-upright position. The least effective learning position is lying on the back. If you place your baby on the floor on his back, he will probably be more interested in cycling with his arms and legs stretched out away from his body. Also, the tonic neck reflex is more dominant when baby is lying on his back, causing his head to turn to one side, his arms to follow, and his hands to stay closed. When you raise your baby to a semi-upright position his arms and legs will come together, touching each other. This stimulates midline play.

Presenting an interesting toy seems to activate baby's whole body as he tries to reach for it. His face and mouth extend toward the object; his feet come up to kick at it or clamp it between them. Baby is beginning to use his whole body to explore his ever widening world. It is important that parents go along with baby's neurological development in encouraging reaching and batting at mobiles. Constantly tempting baby by dangling gadgets over him before he is neurologically ready to reach may overload and frustrate him.

Visual Development

During the third month your baby's visual development leaps ahead. There is more sparkle and recognition in his eyes, especially for parents and familiar caregivers. Notice that your baby will track you, radar-like, as you walk by him and leave the room; he may cry as you depart. He notices movement across the room. He may gaze at beams on the ceiling or plants on a ledge fifteen to twenty feet away. Light and dark contrast is still the most appealing. Babies like to watch shadows on the wall or ceiling and will watch them move as the light source moves. During this stage babies pay more attention to detail. Instead of simply scanning the periphery of objects and persons, they now study the details: the parts of your face, floral patterns, the sofa, etc.

Motor Development

Besides achieving better hand-eye control during the third month, babies also gain better control of the rest of their body movements. Head control improves dramatically during this stage. When pulled up by the hands to a sitting position, babies still show a slight head lag initially, but when sitting erect, they can hold their heads head steady, in the same plane as the rest of their bodies. They may occasionally bob their heads forward or sideways, but they can regain control and again hold them steadily erect.

When lying prone, enjoying some tummy-time, the three-month-old baby will be able to lift his head forty-five to ninety degrees above the floor, high enough to make eye contact momentarily with a parent at the same level. He will then slowly drop his head back down with steady control. When the head is up, in a "search" position, baby can turn his head from side to side, scanning his environment. Mothers have told me that kissing the back of the neck stimulates baby to lift his head. By the third month, babies learn to prop themselves on their flexed forearms, making it easier for them to hold their heads up. Their fists serve as a cushion for the heavy little head when the neck muscles tire. By the third month baby's head spends most of its time higher than his bottom.

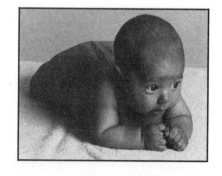

If you hold your baby by his arms, he can sustain most of his weight on his feet for a few moments, using your hands for balance only. When you relax your support, baby sinks slowly to his knees or bottom. (Contrary to old wives' tales, standing your baby up this way does not cause bowed legs; his weight is on his legs for a very short time.) When you hold your baby up against your chest, his improved head and trunk control allow him to push away and peer over your shoulder. For babies, seeing the world from this angle is more satisfying than lying in playpens looking at the ceiling.

While nearly all babies prefer being in your arms, they occasionally enjoy lying on their backs on a carpet or blanket, a position which allows them to kick freely and enjoy being active and alert. You will notice certain movements when your three-month-old baby lies on his back for free-style play. His limbs no longer follow the position of his head all the time (the tonic neck reflex), but instead can swing out freely on both sides while the head stays in the middle. Sometimes babies will bicycle their limbs in a reciprocal fashion; other times they will reach out symmetrically with all four extremities. Smiles and sounds of delight usually accompany this rug play. If you were to raise your baby to a semi-upright position, his hands and legs would meet in front of his body, and the tempo of his movements would lessen.

These newly discovered motor movements may create some problems. During feedings some babies are so distracted by their own body movements that they are unable to wind down long enough to cuddle and suck. Swaddling (wrapping the baby snugly in a receiving blanket) may help to relax the little wiggler long enough to nurse. For most babies, swaddling increases their attentiveness during feedings; others protest being swaddled.

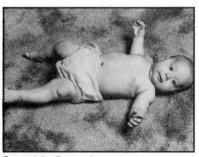
Free-style floor play

Cognitive Development

Patterns or schemas such as "Distress is followed by comfort" are the foundation of a baby's cognitive development. As the baby's central nervous system matures, his patterns of behavior come more under his control, and he begins to make adjustments. He refines these patterns to improve their outcome. For example, by trying various patterns, a baby learns to suck in a way that brings him milk more efficiently. My wife, Martha, noticed that our son Matthew would latch on to the breast, give a few sucks, and then wait for the milk ejection reflex (also known as the let-down) to start the milk flowing. Only then did he start actively sucking and swallowing. He learned that this was an easy way to get a feeding started.

HUNGER
DISCOMFORT — TRIGGERS → Anticipation of Response (Schema)
DISTRESS

Sometime between one and four months of age, the infant discovers the concept of contingency; certain reactions in his environment follow an action of his ("I swipe at the mobile and it moves"). Baby learns cause and effect. This, together with the foundation of trust provided by responsive parents results in a major cognitive developmental milestone: the infant learns that he can have an effect on his environment. He develops a sense of competence, and this leads to self-esteem.

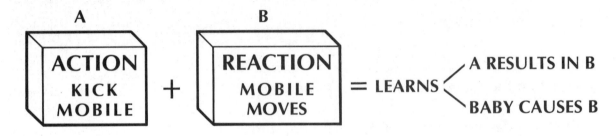

Contingency play

Language Development

During the third month your baby exhibits a lot of body language and can communicate with you more effectively. You and your baby start to have real conversations.

"Matthew and I are starting to have 'talks.' I speak to him in a high-pitched voice and exaggerated inflection with a lot of head nodding. He gets involved in the conversation by waving his arms, cooing, smiling, and using his eyes to express himself. He is very definitely involved in our conversation."

To the delight of his parents, the three-month-old baby responds to his name more consistently. His face beams when you say his name. Since parents naturally put a lot of love into saying their baby's name, it is no wonder that baby soon learns that this sound has special significance. During this stage babies are getting better at locating the source of sounds, often turning their heads toward your voice, even when you are outside their field of vision.

By the third month baby will have developed different cries to signal different needs. You may notice that your baby's cries are interspersed with anticipatory pauses; he expects a response. He also begins to "talk" more. Long strings of goos, gurgles,

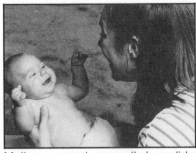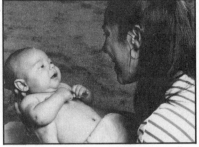

Mother responds promptly to a distress signal, and baby calms and smiles.

hollers, growls, screeches, and sighs proceed from his attempts to make different sounds with different tongue movements. He smacks his lips and clicks his tongue, experimenting with various mouth movements and their results. He still makes only single vowel sounds, but begins to draw them out a bit.

The three-month-old baby also talks more loudly. He experiments with different volumes and amazingly, can adjust his tone of voice to match his parents'. If baby is squealing loudly and you respond by whispering, he is likely to modulate his voice accordingly.

Baby talks while he eats. To a mother's great delight, a three-month-old baby may become so interested in her face that he may frequently pause while nursing, look up at her and smile, and then resume sucking. Your baby may momentarily stop sucking to listen to your voice, depending on how hungry he is or how interesting you are. Or he may look you over and suck at the same time. These little "nursing conversations" convey an "I like to nurse" message.

By three months you can rely on your baby's facial and body language to reveal his emotional state. You can read his eyes, face, and limbs and see pain or contentment. Baby may flap his arms to signal "Pick me up." By reading his mouth and facial gestures, you can tell what emotion is soon to come, either happy or sad. By quickly intervening you can often cause baby to change gears from a cry to a smile. During this stage baby will show recognition in his eyes, his voice, and his behavior. You will feel that he truly knows you, his parents, as special persons in his life.

Infant Stimulation

A recent concept that has gained much attention is infant stimulation, which means setting up environmental events which elicit responses that are pleasing to baby. Infant stimulation programs are being offered in response to parents asking such questions as "What can I do to make my baby, a brighter baby?" Because of the widespread popularity of infant stimulation, I wish to give some parents insight and wisdom on developing a healthy attitude about their baby's play and learning activities.

WHO STIMULATES WHO?

"How can we develop our baby's intelligence?" is a question I hear frequently from new parents. Parents' intense love and pride in their babies make them particularly vulnerable to books and programs that claim to produce brighter babies. As a practicing pediatrician and a father of six (including a toddler), I can sympathize with new parents on this subject. I, too, want to make sure that my baby benefits from all the new research in infant development. I also want to help parents keep a healthy perspective on infant stimulation programs.

Dr. Susan Ludington, founder of the Infant Stimulation Education Association, defines the goal of infant stimulation as a well-rounded, well-balanced baby, one who is equally comfortable and competent in mental, motor, social, and emotional skills.

Here are some things you can do to stimulate your baby's development. These ideas are based on my experience in my practice and my family and on courses I have taken in infant stimulation. They are both practical and fun ways to help you and your baby achieve the goal of all-around development. When used wisely, infant stimulation techniques create a play-learning atmosphere rather than a work-teaching feeling.

Dialoguing with your baby. During the first six months one of the most stimulating activities for your baby is conversation; you both talk and listen to your baby. Dialoguing with your baby fulfills all four "R's" of infant stimulation: rhythm, reciprocity, repetition, and reinforcement. Research has shown that even a newborn responds to his mother's speech and that what may look like a maternal monologue is actually a dialogue: babies react during the pauses in their mothers' speech and the mothers treat those reactions as real conversation. Both mother and baby develop the ability to hold each other's attention, which is an important benefit of infant stimulation. In the first few months mother initiates the sound, and baby responds with his own sounds and gestures. Later, baby initiates and mother responds, which motivates the baby to continue and to improve his skills. The ability to initiate a social exchange empowers babies; it gives them a feeling of competence. When baby is between three and six months of age, he vocalizes and gestures more. When the conversation gets very lively, baby and mother may vocalize in unison (chorusing). Researchers in infant stimulation advise that singing stimulates more of a baby's brain than simply talking. When you sing to your baby, the lyrics are processed by the left half of the brain while the melody affects the right half.

In a dialogue, mother both talks and listens.

Choosing appropriate toys. Classes and toys do not a "superbaby" make. During the first six months, parents are the baby's most important playmates. But even so, toys are a welcome addition to baby's widening world. Try to look at toys from a baby's point of view—what will he enjoy and what is he capable of doing at his stage of development. For example, in the first few months babies are more attracted to contrasting patterns like black and white stripes, dots, bull's-eyes, and checkerboards than they are to pastel pinks and yellows.

Toys for babies between three and six months should be based on the principle of contingency play: what a baby does with the toy produces a reaction, usually sound or movement. Examples include rattles (make sure these are not too big for baby to hold easily) and dangling mobiles or other things to swipe at.

Change toys frequently. Babies get bored with the same old toy. The human face—your face—is an excellent toy for babies. It reacts to what the baby is doing and it is always changing. Perhaps this is why toy bears have become so popular, especially pandas. Their faces don't change like human faces do, but they have a similar pattern of light and dark contrast.

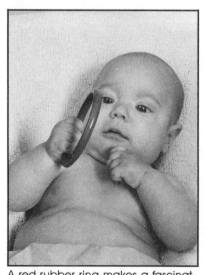

A red rubber ring makes a fascinating toy.

The simplest and most educational toy for a baby around three months of age is a red rubber ring, three to four inches in diameter. Baby can do so much with this simple, inexpensive toy. He can grab it with one hand, bring it to his midline, grab it with the other, pull on it with both hands, release it with one hand while holding on with the other, follow it with his eyes, and gum it when it finds its inevitable destination, baby's mouth. A rubber ring is a simple toy that baby can control completely.

Individualize. Discover which facial gestures, tones of voice, holding positions, and toys please *your* baby. Learn what babies are capable of doing at each stage of development and notice what your baby particularly likes and dislikes doing. I have to confess that as a pediatrician, I look for mothers to tell me what their babies like rather than what they can do. I think this is a more accurate index of mother-baby attachment. Rigid play programs deny your baby's individuality. I encourage parents to pay more attention to what their babies are feeling than to what they are doing. Babies have plenty of time before they have to make their mark on a performance-oriented society.

Watch for "stop signs." Just as babies show signs of being ready for interaction (smiling, eye contact, hands-out gesturing), they also show signs of wanting to stop (vacant staring, turning away, furrowed forehead). Watch for these signs and honor them. Fathers may take longer to recognize these signs than mothers. Because of their eagerness and impatience to play with their babies, fathers may agitate more than stimulate. Because they are seldom allowed the luxury of long periods of unscheduled time with their babies, they tend to rush in to initiate a playful interaction and end up over-stimulating their babies. The best way to approach babies is to follow the look, talk, touch sequence. First establish eye contact with baby, then talk to him, and finally pick him up for play. An important principle for infant stimulation and for all childhood learning is that the most productive interactions are those which are initiated by the baby or child and reinforced by the parents.

Avoid bombardment. Babies have short attention spans, four to ten seconds. Short, frequent playful interactions are more meaningful than longer forced interactions. Find the balance between arousal and settling, a balance which helps the baby get himself organized. Facial games are especially tiring. Watch for signs that baby's attentiveness is waning and that he is losing interest. Learning when not to stimulate and using "attentive stillness" instead is also important to helping your baby develop.

CHOOSING AN INFANT STIMULATION CLASS

I feel that one of the main benefits of classes for infants and toddlers is that many parents and babies get together and have fun. Too often our model of parenting is a mother and a baby alone together at home. But historically mothers have always gotten together to share their work and each other's company. This is healthier for both mothers and babies. Enrolling your baby in an infant stimulation class will have benefits for you, too.

What to look for when choosing a class

1. The program should take an individualized approach to each baby. Rigid programs deny your baby's individuality.

2. The class should emphasize parents and babies enjoying each other. Fun should be more important than performance.

3. The class materials should be appropriate for the age and stage of the babies enrolled.

4. The instructor should have some training in infant stimulation. Ask about his or her credentials.

Course material and information about infant stimulation can be obtained by writing to: Infant Stimulation Education Association; Dr. Susan Ludington, Director; U.C.L.A. Medical Center; Factor 5-942; Los Angeles, CA 90024.

THE PAY-OFF

What's in it for you and for your baby? There is no evidence that fancy toys make brighter babies. When evaluating the influence of toys and programs on infant development, mother still comes out as the most important factor. In the keynote address at a recent annual meeting of the American Academy of Pediatrics, Dr. Michael Lewis discussed the effects of early infant stimulation on later outcome. He concluded that the single most important influence on a child's cognitive development was the mother's responsiveness to her baby's cues. It's not surprising that mother wins again!

I have noticed that parents and babies who engage in stimulating activities together show mutual sensitivity and trust. Researchers in infant development are widening their focus and realizing that when parents and baby spend more time doing things together, the baby also helps the parents develop. Infant stimulation classes help you know and appreciate your infant's capabilities and preferences at each stage of development. Because the more you interact with your baby and the more he responds to you, the more you want to continue this interaction, these programs might better be called "parent stimulation." Infant stimulation activities, whether in a class setting or at home on your living room floor, help you achieve two basic goals of early parenting: to know your baby and to help your baby feel right. If you achieve these two goals you are well on your way to a lifetime of enjoying your child.

SUMMARY: *TWO TO THREE MONTHS*

Large motor

• Lifts head more than forty-five degrees, turns it from side to side when lying on tummy; lifts chest, rests on elbows and forearms.

• Slight head lag when pulled to sit; can hold head steady when sitting.

• Sits erect when supported at hips, but head bobs a bit; slumps forward when support is removed.

Fine motor

• Hands open most of the time; holds and shakes rattle, grabs onto clothing, hair.

• Looks at hand in front of face; grabs one hand with the other, sucks fists.

• Begins to bring arms to midline to encircle toy.

• Swipes at and reaches for dangling objects; more misses than hits.

Language/ social

- Different cries for different needs; cries have anticipatory pauses.
- Vocalizes when spoken to; waves arms and smiles.
- Pauses, looks up, and smiles during feedings.
- Sounds are louder and more drawn out.
- Face expresses emotion: bigger, whole-body smiles, may laugh occasionally; frowns, grimaces.
- Flaps arms to signal "pick me up."

Cognitive

- Orients toward voice of approaching person
- Scans and studies mouth, eyes of parent's face; pays more attention to detail.
- Face lights up, recognizes parent.
- Contingency play—learning about cause and effect.

CHAPTER SEVEN: THE FOURTH MONTH

Responsive

The first three months of a baby's life are the "fitting in" stage when baby learns two fundamental lessons: organization and trust. If his needs are met consistently and his cues read accurately, baby learns to fit into the environment and a feeling of rightness results. With this foundation, baby can begin to interact with his care-giving world in more meaningful ways. His social skills start to develop during the second and third months and really blossom during the next stage, the interaction stage, from four to six months.

By the fourth month, most parents feel completely connected to their babies. The social development of the four-month-old can be summarized in one word: responsive. Babies this age can concentrate longer on visual and motor activities. Four-month-olds look at you longer, play more with their hands, and talk in longer "sentences." They are better able to entertain their caregivers with social exchanges. They are also more interested in their environment. During earlier months babies discover that "I fit." In the fourth month, it seems as if babies decide that "because I fit, I'm going to enjoy it."

Visual Development

During the fourth month babies reach an important visual milestone. They develop binocular vision, the ability to use both eyes together. This means that your baby has depth perception, the ability to judge the distance between himself and the things he sees. The development of binocular vision is a prelude to the next hand-eye skill, visually directed reaching—being able to reach out and grab the things he sees. Binocular vision also enables your baby to see you more clearly at greater distances. His intimate space (the distance at which baby sees clearly enough to sustain his interest) increases to at least three feet. This improved vision allows your baby to get a clear image of your whole body, not just your face. He will notice your hand and arm gestures, and they help to hold his attention and improve his language skills.

DEVELOPMENT OF TRACKING AND GAZING

Most four-month-old babies have mastered the skill of tracking a moving object for a full 180 degrees from side to side, although they still use mainly their eyes to follow objects and their heads have to catch up. By the fourth month most babies can see, locate, and track an object that is a few feet away nearly as well as an adult. (Even adults often track first with their eyes and then turn their heads to catch up.) Since the eyes see more clearly when looking straight ahead, baby will soon learn that it is better to move his eyes and head simultaneously when following a moving object. This is called **gazing**.

Gazing is more than just seeing. Seeing involves the eye and the associated nerve structures that are required to produce an image. Gazing encompasses the sense of sight plus the skills of head and eye rotation which help baby keep his vision fixed on an object. The interaction of vision and motor skills makes it possible for the four-month-old to take in or tune out his world as he wishes. If he is dis-pleased by what he sees, his ability to gaze allows him to "change channels" by turning his head. When you hold your baby so that he can look at you face to face, you'll notice that he gazes straight ahead at you. If you change his position so that he is looking in another direction, you'll see him tilt his head back and around in order to continue gazing at you.

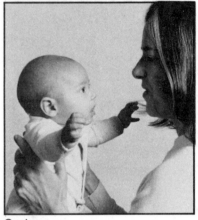

Gazing

The visual-motor system develops earlier than loco-motor skills in humans. Compared to most animals, human babies are relatively slow to develop locomo-tor skills. The ability to interact with the caregiver is more crucial to the survival of a human baby. Eye-to-eye contact helps human babies "capture" what they need most—the love of their caregivers.

"One of the most exciting things about our four-month-old's development is the way he reaches for me with his eyes. He expresses thanks with his eyes. He turns his face and eyes up toward me. They are so expressive and adoring. He appears to be fully aware of me as his source of love, nourishment, and well-being. He craves my presence and totally enjoys our togetherness. It's a love affair, full-blown. I recognize the love in his eyes as one more emotion that he's capable of expressing."

Around the fourth month babies show increasing interest in colors. They prefer natural colors like the reds and yellows of spring flowers and are least interested in pastel colors (like those used to decorate most traditional nurseries). To encourage baby's interest in color, continue to contrast light and dark colors; for example, your baby will pay more attention to red stripes if they are next to yellow stripes.

Hearing Skills

Development of voice localization and recognition. By the fourth month most babies can consistently associate the sound with the location of the speaker. When you enter the room and call baby's name, he will acknowledge your greeting by turning in the direction of your voice. He expects the voice and person to go together. Babies often become upset when they hear a parent's voice but cannot see the source. For this reason, it is better to make eye contact with your baby before you speak to him. Don't be worried if your baby doesn't always turn towards your voice. Babies can selectively tune out one stimulus in preference for another. This allows them to concentrate on one thing at a time and also to avoid overload when they are bombarded with too much sensory input. For example, if baby is concentrating on looking at an interesting person or activity, you could talk right into his ear and he might not acknowledge you.

This improvement in voice recognition and localization can help calm a fussy baby. When your baby is fussing in another room, sing out "Mama's coming." He will often quiet down and will be waving his arms and kicking his legs in anticipation of your entrance when you enter the room.

Babies this age also begin to turn toward familiar household sounds: the phone ringing, doors slamming. They may interrupt a feeding to acknowledge a familiar voice, such as when dad comes home and says "Hi, baby." Sometime around four to six months baby will begin to follow dinner table conversations, turning toward and attending to various speakers around the table. The four-month-old is on his way to becoming a good communicator because he is learning how to listen.

Motor Development

Increasing hand play is the most interesting motor milestone of baby's fourth month. Playing with his hands in front of his face becomes the usual mode of self-entertainment. You will notice that your baby spends a lot of time sucking on his fingers and fists. During this stage babies show a natural tendency to draw their hands and feet toward each other and toward the mouth. Also, sucking needs often intensify during the fourth month to relieve the pain of teething, and baby learns to gnaw on his hands as readily available teething rings. Increased drooling and gum soreness are other signs of the onset of teething.

Baby may spend several minutes just contemplating his fingers as well as exploring them with his mouth. The position of baby's hands can give parents some cues. If baby's hands are folded together in a meditative position, he may be content to spend some time in self-amusement. If the hands are wide open or are reaching up and out, interpret this as a sign that baby is inviting you to play or is asking you to pick him up. When your baby is very alert, excited, or interested, his hands will be wide open, with one or both arms extended up, and you will definitely get the feeling that he is trying to talk to you with his hands.

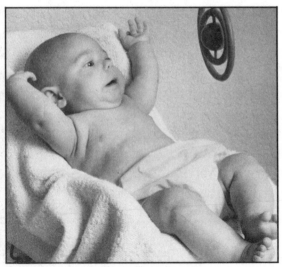

Baby meditates on his fingers.

Gathering-in: reaching with both arms.

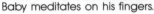

HAND PLAY

When your baby is sitting propped up in an infant seat, his hands will usually be together, fingers interlocked in prayer-like fashion, and he will fold and unfold his hands and fingers to amuse himself. When a rubber ring is placed in his hand, he grasps it mitten-like, all the fingers working together to hold the ring against his palm without using the thumb. Sometimes the other hand comes across and also grasps the ring. Baby may let go of the ring with the first hand and accidentally transfer the ring to the other hand, much to his own amazement. Hand-to-mouth play gets at least equal time with hand-to-hand play. Most of the time objects placed in baby's hand find their way to his mouth before they make it to the other hand.

Gathering-in. The gathering-in motion that babies exhibit at this stage is a prelude to mature reaching. If you dangle or hold an interesting object (a rattle or a ring) in front of your baby within the range of his hands, he probably will not grasp or reach for it, but instead will bring his arms together and try to embrace it, as if to gather it in toward himself. Sometimes he will succeed. Sometimes he'll miss the object entirely, and his embracing hands will meet and end up in his mouth. If you move the toy beyond baby's reach, he will quickly lose interest in the game. If you move the toy while he is reaching for it, he will probably miss it and turn away because you have violated the rules of the reaching game. He cannot yet make "in-flight" corrections, especially if the toy moves out of focus or out of reach. Four-month-old babies still like to play "sit and hit" games. Hold your baby in your lap or place him upright in an infant seat at a thirty to forty-five degree angle. Dangle his favorite mobile within hitting range. Notice that he often reaches toward the toy with his head and mouth before his hands. At this age babies may spend five or ten minutes taking little jabs and swipes at objects as they try out their newly developed hand-eye skills.

LOCOMOTOR SKILLS

During the fourth month babies develop more control over their movements. When lying on their backs, they assume a more symmetric posture, both arms and both legs out to the side instead of the one-arm-out, one-arm-in position so characteristic of younger babies. The effect of the tonic neck reflex on posture has almost completely disappeared at this stage, allowing babies more control over their limbs.

Your baby will occasionally be in a "motor mood." He doesn't want to be held or played with, but wants to be put down on his back on a rug or blanket and left to do his own thing in freestyle movements. He will thrust out his arms and legs, cycle his limbs, and wave his arms as if he is flapping his wings.

POSTURE

Head control is much steadier during this stage. When placed on their tummies, four-month-olds will prop themselves up on both arms and lift their heads to nearly a ninety-degree angle, chest off the floor, and sustain this position long enough to look around or carry on a short conversation. When pulled up by the hands to a sitting position, the head lags only slightly and when held sitting erect, it no longer bobs. Babies this age are able to hold their heads steady and look up, down, and around long enough to carry on a social exchange without tiring.

Early sitting postures. When placed in the sitting position, baby can prop himself up with his hands only momentarily before falling forward on his nose. His upper back is straight, but his lower back muscles are still too weak to allow him to sit upright. Your baby has to develop a sense of balance in the sitting position. If he feels himself falling to one side, he will thrust out his arm on that side to catch his fall. A good test of the emerging strength of baby's back muscles is to hold the baby's legs while he is sitting. Baby can balance himself momentarily in this position, but will soon topple over because of his weak lower back muscles and primitive sense of balance.

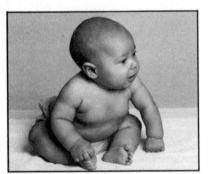

The four-month-old can sit propped on his hands for a few moments before toppling over.

Baby likes to stand, supported by your hands. If you momentarily let go, he can sustain his weight for one to two seconds before his trunk and legs slowly collapse. When you let go, he tries to balance by flinging his arms out to each side. When held in a supported standing position, baby likes to push up his own weight with his legs. He soon collapses and then pushes up again. The delight in his face tells you that he enjoys this newly discovered skill.

Rolling over may begin around four months of age, although this tends to be one of the most variable milestones in a baby's development. Babies this age may roll from back to side, from side to side, or even from tummy to back. Most babies roll from tummy to back before rolling from back to tummy. The age at which a baby rolls over seems to be more a matter of infant temperament than developmental maturity. Very active babies tend to roll over sooner. When lying on their backs, they may lurch over to one side if they're curious about what is over there. When they're on their tummies, pushing up their chests with their hands, active babies may throw their head to one side, surprising themselves as they flip over onto their backs. The persistent squirmer may flip over and over like a flapping fish, making diapering a challenge. Less active babies are more content to amuse themselves on their backs or tummies without any interest in rolling over for another month or two.

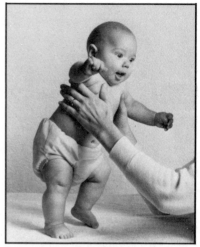

Balancing while standing supported.

You can increase your appreciation of your baby's development by observing and writing down the sequence he goes through when beginning a certain play activity. For example:

1. Rattle dangled within grasping distance.

2. Arms start moving and body is excited.

3. Accepts rattle when placed in hand.

4. Looks at rattle for a few moments.

5. Brings rattle toward mouth or toward body to explore with free hand.

To learn about your baby's development you must be more than a parental videocamera. Look for subtle changes in your baby's activities. Notice not only the sequential actions, but also the facial expressions and body language and the feelings they convey during and after a certain play activity. This ability to observe your baby early on sets the stage for interpreting his behavior as a toddler, an ability which is very important to discipline.

The increasing visual awareness and head movements of the four-month-old may necessitate a change in the way you hold him. In the first few months babies are content to nestle against their

HOLDING PATTERNS

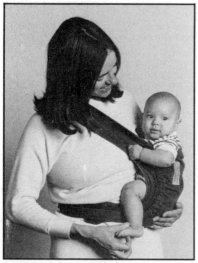
Older babies prefer baby carriers that allow them to see.

parents' chests. But as they get older they want to see where they are. They may protest any restriction that doesn't allow them to turn their heads a full 180 degrees to take in all the visual delights of the widening world. Use a baby carrier that allows nearly all of baby's head to be exposed, so he can look around as he pleases. Some carriers can be used with baby facing forward or riding on your hip, giving him a good vantage point. When you're not using a carrier, hold your alert baby straddling your hip, facing outward while sitting on your hip, or bent and seated on your arm, facing forward. The forward carrying position is ideal when baby is in the quiet alert mood and interested in relating to his environment.

SAFETY AWARENESS

Your baby's increasing motor skills, especially his ability to scoot and roll over, dictate that you become increasingly aware of safety during the fourth month. Changing table and infant seat accidents are particularly common at this stage. Never leave a baby unattended on a changing table, countertop, or any other surface from which he could roll off. When sitting in infant seats, four-month-old babies can thrust their feet or arms with such momentum that they can slide or roll out of the seat if not properly secured. After the third or fourth month, it is wise to place the seat only on a secure well-padded surface such as a carpeted floor, and use the seat's safety belt. The reaching and grabbing tendencies of the curious four-month-old make him particularly likely to pull on potentially harmful objects, such as the hot cup of coffee in your hand or on the table. Never place hot beverages within reach of a baby. No matter how careful you are in holding your hot cup of coffee, your baby can reach up and pull it down on himself when you are momentarily looking away. The result can be a serious burn.

Cognitive Development

During this stage the rapid development of the central nervous system results in improved visual acuity, better head control, and more directed arm and hand movements. All of these complement baby's cognitive development, and allow him to develop and refine new patterns of behavior. For example, baby can now gaze at mother from a distance of a few feet, so he develops a mental image of her looks, her smiles, her sounds. His new smiles help to hold mother's attention longer, and from the new social experiences, baby develops a schema of mother as a social person as well as a source of comfort. He also learns that as mother moves slowly from one side of him to the other, he can move his eyes and head to sustain the interaction. However, if mother moves out of sight baby loses her altogether because he does not yet have the ability to remember and reproduce her image in his mind. Either he will fuss because the schema or "groove" that he was in is gone, or he will switch on another schema, such as comforting himself by thumb-sucking.

To me it seems as if an infant's developing mind is like the making of a record with the patterns of behavior being set down as grooves. The baby, then, can periodically click into one of the grooves that has been set.

A different pattern of behavior is called up when father enters. Father looks different, smells different, sounds different. He gives and responds to social cues differently. Matthew learned certain behavior patterns that were associated only with me. Almost every day during his early months we would take a walk together. I would hold him against my chest and position his head under my chin, a position I call the neck nestle, and then start singing and walking. After a few months of this, Matthew would immediately nestle into this "groove" when I picked him up in anticipation of the song and walk which were soon to follow. (During his second year Matthew added the word "go" to this pattern of behavior.)

At first baby's patterns of behavior center around his own body or his caregiver's body. Becoming able to use his hands as tools facilitates a giant leap in cognitive development: baby now learns to *decide* what to do with his hands. Now that he can reach and grab he has to make decisions as to when and how to reach and what to do with an object once he has grabbed it. This will eventually lead to another cognitive refinement: accommodation. In later months baby will use his mind to help his hands make in-flight corrections during reaching so that he can grasp objects better.

Branching out is another important feature of cognitive development at this stage. The infant uses one master skill—the ability to reach out and grab a toy—to branch out into other skills, such as manipulating the toy once he has grabbed it.

The infant is not just a passive player during these early stages of cognitive development. He takes a very active part in engaging and holding the attention of his caregivers. The more sensitively these caregivers respond, the more the infant is stimulated to refine those cues which engage and hold a caregiver's attention. It seems that much of an infant's intellectual development is tied to this early attachment relationship.

Social Skills

The ability to initiate and respond to social exchanges is the main developmental landmark of the fourth month. To help you better interpret your baby's early social signals, try the following: list baby's signals in one column and what he is trying to tell you (or what you think he is trying to tell you) in an adjacent column. Here's an example (the list would, of course, be different for each baby):

Signals

1. Short, breathy, stacatto cries
2. Smacking lips and clutching at Mom's blouse
3. Fusses and arches back when held
4. Fusses when put down on rug

What baby's trying to tell you

1. "I'm going to cry unless you pick me up right away."
2. "I want to nurse."
3. "I want to be put down on the rug to kick and play."
4. "I want to be walked around, held in the baby carrier."

Do this again next month, and as you get better at reading your baby's signals, add a third column recording how he reacts to your response to his cue. This exercise will help you improve your ability to read and respond to your baby's signals. Giving your baby an appropriate response to his signals motivates him to refine his communication ability.

Feeding and sleeping patterns. While the term feeding schedule is still not in the vocabulary of most four-month-olds, some babies do settle down to a somewhat predictable, although inconsistent, feeding schedule at this age. Babies will often give up one of the night feedings by the fourth month. Most breastfed babies will still wake up for at least one middle-of-the-night feeding. Bottle-fed babies may often sleep a five- or six-hour stretch by the fourth month.

If your baby has not settled into a predictable nap routine by the fourth month, here are some scheduling suggestions for tired parents. (Naps are just as important for mothers as they are for babies.) Many alert and active babies do not seem to need a long nap during the day, but their mothers certainly do. Choose one or two times during the day that you need a nap, usually late morning or late afternoon. Take your baby into your bedroom and nestle down with your baby on the bed next to you. Cuddle your baby close, and if you're breastfeeding, nurse him. Reinforce this sleep-inducing atmosphere with soothing tapes or records. Soon one or both of you will be asleep. (Use a guard rail or pillows or push your bed against the wall to make sure that baby can't roll off while you're asleep.) If your baby is not in the mood for a nap at the same time you are, he may initially fuss and squirm, but he will soon get the message that this time and this setting is for napping. It may take you two weeks of doing this every day to get your baby into a predictable nap routine, but be patient—it does work. A word of advice to tired and busy mothers: when baby falls asleep you may be tempted to sneak away and finally get some work done. Resist this temptation and nap with your baby. When there's a new baby in the house, your need for rest takes priority over other household obligations.

Things to do with a four-month-old

1. Sofa sitting. Sit baby in the bend of a sofa pillow. He will spend five to ten minutes looking around and enjoying this new posture and vantage point.

2. Sit and hit games. Dangle an interesting toy or mobile within baby's reach. He'll punch at it or try to gather it into his arms.

3. Grab and shake games. Offer rattles, rings, rag dolls, blankets.

4. Peek-a-boo. This old favorite can be played by moving in and out of baby's visual field or by hiding behind a

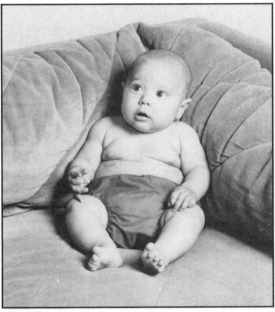

Sofa sitting

Mirror play

piece of cloth or cardboard. Be sure to talk to your baby and make exaggerated faces. ("Where's mommy? Here I am!")

5. Kick toys. Pom-poms, a helium balloon on a short string, rattles, and pleasant noise makers can be attached to baby's ankles for him to activate with his kicking. He can also kick at mobiles or balls within range.

6. Finger games. Give your baby piles of yarn to explore with his fingers. Change the texture by using different kinds of yarn. Tying yarn loosely to baby's fingers helps him realize that he can move each of these interesting appendages separately. Later, lightweight puppet figures can be attached to the yarn. Never leave a baby unattended with a piece of string or yarn.

7. Rolling games. Drape baby over a large beach ball and roll it slowly back and forth. This helps him develop balance.

8. Pull-up games. Hold a thin bar, such as a golf club, in front of baby's chest. He will grab on, tighten his grip, and gradually pull himself up.

9. Mirror play. Babies love to sit or be held in front of mirrors so that they can watch their own movements.

10. Splash, splash. Baby's newly discovered arm power makes bath play fun.

11. Massage your baby.

12. "Gitchee-gitchee-goo." Tickling games which use tactile and vocal gestures will get you both laughing.

Language: Four to Six Months

During the first three months babies learn to enjoy language and the responses they receive from their caregivers. This enjoyment is the basis for their acquisition of more advanced language skills. During the next stage, babies learn that language is a pleasurable behavior in itself and that it gives pleasure to others and has an important impact on their environment.

VOCALIZATION

In the early months, baby's relatively small oral cavity was filled by his large tongue. This accounts for the nasal quality of baby's early sounds. Most of these early sounds emanated from the back of the throat and came out sounding like "g." This is why baby's early language is often interpreted as sounding like "goo-goo."

From the fourth to the sixth month the oral cavity enlarges, allowing the tongue and lips to participate more in sound production. Sounds begin to come from the front of the mouth as well as the back. Baby also begins to use his mouth to modify these sounds; he may begin vocalizing with a wide-mouthed "ah" sound and then close his mouth a bit to change it to "oh." The resulting sound almost gives the impression that baby is telling you what he feels. The sounds begin to take on a predictable pattern, creating the impression that baby is talking to you. For example, "ah" may mean "I'm excited"; "oh" means "I like this little sound that I can produce simply by moving my mouth a bit."

Babies take great delight in recognizing that they can change the quality of the sound by moving their mouths. Expressive language begins. In response to pleasing social stimuli, such as kisses and tickles, baby lets out short chuckles which grow into true laughter. You will begin to associate certain vocalizations with specific activities. In anticipation of nursing, baby may come out with a string of short vowel-like syllables ("Ah-ah-ah") interspersed with some breathy sounds and rapid inhaling and exhaling. In response to other exciting stimuli, your baby may produce longer sounds by stretching out his vowels ("Eeeee!").

Babies are not the only ones who get excited about their growing capacity for speech. It's exciting for parents, too. You can begin to listen to what baby says and how he says it to get clues to what baby is feeling. Better coordination between baby's respiratory system and his larynx (voice box) enables him to modulate the pitch of his voice and produce more intense, high-pitched sounds. Protests and attention-getting yells become louder and seem to trigger a more rapid response from his listeners. Laughter becomes funnier as baby lets out a crescendo of squeals lasting five to ten seconds. The excitement of this early baby talk is most noticeable during play. When really excited, baby pushes the air through his quivering little vocal cords so fast that his laughter is full of high-pitched squeals which, when taken in the context of a radiant smiling face, indicate pleasure. Short, staccato, breathy cries of increasing intensity are usually clues to some pressing need; if not properly attended to, they will progress into all-out wailing.

Baby also experiments with a variety of bubble-blowing sputters called "raspberries." These are his first attempt to modify his vocal sounds with his lips. Because of his saliva-filled throat (the pre-teething stage), these vocalizations can get pretty wet.

All these new sounds last longer, too. During these stretched-out coos, baby continuously changes the shape of his mouth, as if testing each sound for the effect it has on listeners and how it sounds to him. The four- to six-month-old baby is becoming more interested in his own sounds and may not always stop to listen to you converse with him.

Sometime between four and six months babies start to make the earliest of true language sounds—babbling, the sounds produced when baby combines a vowel sound with a consonant and repeats them over and over ("Ba-ba-ba"). His babbling ability matures through the rest of the first year. (See the section on language development in the six-to-nine-month chapter.)

A "good morning" speech

To really appreciate how rudimentary sounds progress into intelligible speech, you might want to tape-record your baby's sounds at various ages. By listening to these recordings you will be able to pick out certain repetitive patterns, such as the comforting sounds of "ah" or the excitement of "Eeeee!" In my own family we have found that it's easiest to tape baby's vocalizations when he first wakes up. These delightful wake-up sounds announce to the world that today's play is about to begin. This is also a time when responsive smiling is at its peak. In response to a happy greeting ("Good morning, baby!") your baby's smile builds up to an ear-to-ear grin accompanied by lots of wiggles and expressive sounds. Baby wants someone to look at him so that he can smile and talk back.

BODY LANGUAGE

Communication skills involve both sounds and body movements, and body language, along with vocal skill, begins to mature rapidly beginning in the fourth month. This new body language, added to the interesting sounds of the four-to-six-month-old, makes this an important stage for the learning of social interaction. Babies learn that language is primarily a behavior to be enjoyed, not just a skill to be mastered.

Mutual gazing. Between three and six months of age, babies become able to control their neck muscles, which allows them to choose what they want to look at. A baby can now initiate social interactions because he is better able to align his face with that of the person speaking to him and can maintain a longer gaze. Baby orients his head toward yours, smiles, wiggles, vocalizes, and with these cues, invites a social exchange. He is able to initiate, maintain, or stop a social interaction by simply moving his head.

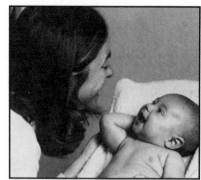
Mutual gazing

Mutual gazing is a potent interpersonal magnet. Adults seldom hold a mutual gaze for more than a few seconds, except perhaps when falling in love. However, parents and babies' mutual gaze can remain interlocked for much longer. I have seen babies gaze at their caregivers, trance-like, for up to thirty seconds. They nearly always outlast their caregivers at the blinking game, holding their eyes focused and motionless much longer than the adult.

Mutual gazing also allows you to read your baby's non-verbal cue that he needs a change in the level of social interaction. If baby turns his head and his eyes away from you, this is a stop signal. When baby's eyes take on a glazed look, this is a signal that baby is either not ready for or is tiring of the interaction. If baby's head is aligned with yours and his eyes are still wide open but focused on something else, interpret it as if baby is saying to you, "Hold that thought—I'll be right back with you as soon as I finish looking at this interesting lamp." The ability to engage and disengage in social interchanges is one of the most exciting behaviors of the four-to-six-month stage.

Gesturing is the next exciting language behavior that begins during this stage. Gestures are one of the most important forerunners of verbal language because they are replaced later on by their equivalent in words. Baby may point or reach toward an object or person, and this same behavior will eventually be replaced or accompanied by verbal requests.

Matching is another interesting language ability which develops during this stage. Baby makes primitive, babbling attempts to match your sounds and body language. This capability indicates that infant speech is an intelligent activity in which baby recognizes and voluntarily attempts to reproduce audible and visual language.

Crying usually diminishes between four and six months as baby learns to communicate with his caregivers using other vocal and body signs. How soon and to what degree baby replaces crying with other language depends a great deal on whether baby has learned to trust his caregiving environment. The more responsive parents are to both crying and non-crying language during the first three months, the sooner baby will substitute a more pleasant style of communication for crying. You will begin to notice that your baby is learning which sounds and gestures elicit a caregiving response. If you do not respond to your baby's cues until they have escalated into all-out crying, he is less likely to replace that crying with other communication signals.

ENCOURAGING YOUR BABY'S LANGUAGE DEVELOPMENT

Taking an active part in helping your baby enjoy language not only helps baby learn to communicate better; it also helps you as parents to communicate better with your baby. Learning about your baby helps you learn from your baby.

Use familiar openers. Open a social exchange with familiar words, such as the baby's name, and repeat them frequently with a musical quality in your voice. By four months, most babies respond consistently to their names. At this age baby will also notice words that obviously refer only to him, such as "Cutie" or "Sweetie;" he recognizes the unique tone of voice that you reserve for him. To observe how important baby's name is to him, try this test:

talk to him from behind without using his name, then speak the same sentence prefacing it with his name. Baby will turn toward the speaker more consistently if he hears his name. Babies love repetitive rhymes and poems which feature their names: "My name is Daniel; I'm not a cocker spaniel."

Babies tune into conversations and can tune them out as well. Use opening words such as "hi" and "hello" to engage baby's attention and hold it throughout the conversation. When you notice your baby's gaze begin to wander repeat these opening cue words to re-engage baby.

Labeling. Give names to familiar toys, persons, or household pets. Start with one-syllable words such as Mom, Dad, ball, cat. When your baby's gaze indicates that he is interested in the cat, teach him the name for it. First use an opening phrase ("Hi, baby!") to engage baby's attention. Once baby turns from the cat and locks in on your gaze, slowly turn your face toward the cat, allowing baby to follow your eyes. When both of you are looking at the cat, point and exclaim "cat" in a very excited tone. During this stage of development baby associates the label "cat" with the whole sequence of events—your steering his gaze toward the cat, your pointing at the cat, and your saying the word "cat." He probably will not turn toward the cat if you give him only the label without the accompanying directing gestures. In the next developmental stage, from six to nine months, baby may turn and point toward the cat as it walks by with no more cues from you other than saying the word "cat."

Expand on baby-initiated language. Expansion carries labeling one step further. When baby initiates an interest in a familiar object, for example, gazing at the cat walking by, expand on his interest by exclaiming, "There's cat!" Expansion capitalizes on a well-known principle of learning: learning that is

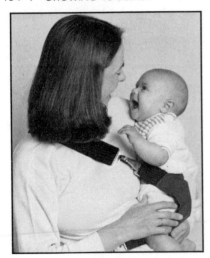

initiated by the baby is more likely to be remembered. Follow through on other baby-initiated cues. When baby sneezes, quickly exclaim "Bless you!" After many repetitions of this response, baby will quickly turn towards you after a sneeze, anticipating your exclamation. Expansion and following through reinforce baby's emerging sense of competency, making him feel that his primitive language has value and therefore that he himself has value.

Echoing. Another way to capitalize on baby-initiated language is to echo the sound back to baby. Mimicking the sounds that baby produces further reinforces that you hear what he says and are interested in his sounds.

Taking turns. Remember that a dialogue has a rhythm of listening and responding. Try to develop a rhythm in your conversations with your baby. Encouraging him to listen is an important part of language development. Taking turns in conversation fosters attentive stillness, an important quality in language-learning. This is the state in which baby is most receptive to learning about language. Taking an active part in helping your baby enjoy language not only helps baby learn to communicate better. It also helps parents communicate with their baby. Learning about your baby helps you learn from your baby.

SUMMARY: *THREE TO FOUR MONTHS*

Large motor

- Tonic neck reflex disappears; can use arms in midline play; more freestyle movement.
- Lifts head ninety degrees when lying on tummy, chest completely off floor; rotates head.
- Getting ready to roll over; at first, usually tummy to back.
- No sagging at knees when supported in standing position. Sits erect when supported; minimal head lag when pulled to sit.
- Sits propped forward on extended arms.

Fine motor

- Brings toy in hand to midline; brings toy to mouth; may accidentally switch toy from one hand to the other.
- Two-handed reaching; gathers in toy directly in front of him.
- Begins subtle pointing.
- Swipes at dangling objects are still usually misses.

Language/ social

- Produces predictable sound patterns in response to different stimuli.
- Changes mouth to change character of sounds ("ah-oh").
- Squealing laughter, "raspberries."
- Language and gestures are more expressive; hands express receptiveness to stimulation.
- Listens to self; attends to dinner table conversation.
- Gaping, wide open smiles.

Cognitive

- Localizes familiar voices, even outside of field of vision.
- Tracks moving persons; gazes at interesting objects across room.
- Mutual gazing; reads parent's facial gestures.
- Likes sit-and-hit games, peek-a-boo, grab-and-shake toys, rolling on beach ball, tickling.

CHAPTER EIGHT: THE FIFTH MONTH

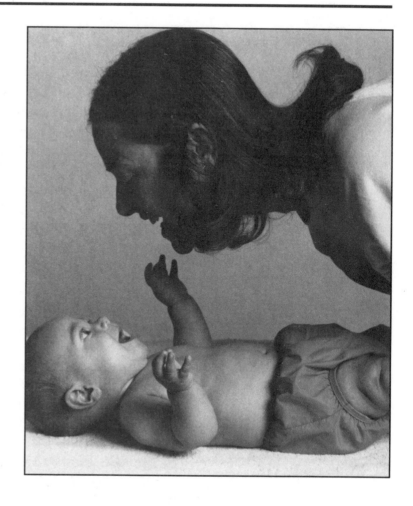

Reaching Out

During the fifth month, babies' visual and motor systems reach a major developmental milestone: visually directed reaching. Babies can finally reach out and grab objects and persons that are within reaching distance. They become manipulators of objects. Baby reaches for a rattle, turns it, shakes it, studies it, and then brings the object to his mouth.

The Reaching Sequence

One of the most interesting developmental progressions during the first six months is the sequence of steps that baby goes through in learning to reach out and handle the world around him. During the first couple of months baby learns to "reach" with his eyes. If the object or person is interesting enough to sustain his interest, baby's head bobs toward the object and his hands wave and dart out, seemingly without direction, but as if he is thinking, "There's something interesting out there that I want to get." If you watch baby's hands during this formative stage you will notice that now and again a finger momentarily points or darts out in the direction of the object of interest. This subtle, almost imperceptible gesture is the beginning of reaching.

The next developmental milestone in the reaching sequence occurs around three months of age when baby discovers that his hands are easily reachable objects and that, even more amazingly, they are part of himself. He begins pointing, swiping, and batting at close objects. His hit rate is variable, and his misses usually outnumber the direct hits. There's very little directionality in the early swiping movements. The beginning of midline play (using the hands in front of the body) is another important milestone in the development of reaching. One hand serves as the target for the other. Also at this stage, the hands open up, and baby develops the ability to see more clearly, further motivating him to reach out. All these things work together to enable baby to perform gathering-in motions. His reaching efforts take on directionality.

Around the fifth month, one-handed reaching begins. The initial touch-grasp motion is rather primitive with baby using his whole hand in a mitten-like grasp to trap the object between all of his fingers and the palm of his hand. Prior to this stage, baby would reach for and grasp only objects that were brought within an inch or two of the hand. Around the fifth month, baby will reach out with one hand for objects that are nearly an arm's length away. He will grasp the intended toy precisely in his hand, examine it, and then transfer it to the other hand or to his mouth.

From the fifth month onward, babies refine their reaching abilities. At first, when your baby reaches for an object such as a block, his hand does not adjust to the shape of the block until he is actually touching it. As he grows older you may notice that his hand slows up as he reaches the object and his fingers open to accommodate the shape of the object before he makes contact. (This is most easily seen in slow-motion films of the reaching sequence.) In later months this ability will become even more refined, and baby will be able to make in-flight adjustments in order to grab a moving object. This reflects the increasing maturity of baby's visual-motor system.

Baby can use his newly refined reaching ability to show which toys he likes and also to show dislikes. For example, he may swipe at your arm or push your hand away from his mouth when you attempt to give him medicine.

Reaching for a toy

Visual Development

Eyes fixed on the tree

One of the reasons that babies can reach better at five months is because they can see better. They can now take in the visual delights of an entire room. When you hold your baby you will notice that he pulls away from your shoulder and scans the whole room. His eyes may fix for several moments on a distant contrasting object such as a dark beam on a white ceiling. He also pays more attention to the wonders of nature: moving tree branches and how the sun casts shadows. Baby begins to be interested in what you're looking at; he looks where you look.

At this age, out of sight is out of mind. If baby drops the rattle he has been holding, he pursues it visually until it is out of sight and then quickly loses interest. Not until a few months later will he realize that a disappearing object still exists even if he can't see it. Baby also tracks disappearing persons more consistently at this stage. When mom or dad or any other familiar caregiver gets up and leaves the room, baby's eyes will follow until that person is out of sight. He may then vocalize his disappointment at being left behind or may turn his visual interest toward another person or object.

Babies begin to be fascinated with small objects at this age. Their eyes may fixate on a small pellet, such as a raisin, but usually they make no attempts to pick up or rake in the small object.

COLOR PREFERENCE

The previous preference for black and white gives way to a liking for colors, especially for contrasting reds and yellows. The increasing attention to contrasts and details prompts baby to show momentary interest in story books, especially those with large letters and pictures on a light background. Your baby may scan and study a page intently and make accompanying cooing noises.

Motor Development

When lying down the five-month-old flaps his arms, pedals his legs, rocks on his tummy, and arches his neck, playing "airplane." He may become frustrated at not being able to take off. If you place your hands against the soles of his feet while he is doing this, he may be able to propel himself forward by pushing off from your hands. All this motion is in anticipation of crawling; baby makes these movements in the air before he makes them on the ground. Baby can now lift his chest off the floor with his arms extended straight out as props, pushing up more with his hands than his forearms. In this position he may begin drawing up one leg in preparation for crawling. Place your hands against his toes and allow him to push off and discover his first mode of self-propulsion. If you claim his attention from the side while he is practicing the push-up position, he may momentarily balance on one arm as he reaches for you.

When lying on his back, baby cranes his neck forward to see his flying feet. He may grab and play with his toes and even suck on them a while. When pulling baby up by the hands to the sitting position, he assists you by lifting his head forward and flexing his elbows. Still unable to sit without support, baby leans forward propped on both arms, peering at and sometimes grabbing his toes. He gradually lifts one hand and arm to reach for an object, maintaining his balance with the other arm.

ROLLING OVER

The ability to use his hands and elbows to push himself up allows baby to roll from tummy to back. Watch your baby's rolling-over sequence: he pushes himself up, pushing higher with one arm, and then leans his head and shoulders backwards and towards the side, his head acting as a sort of fly-

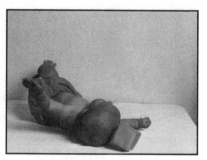

Rolling from tummy to back

wheel increasing his twisting momentum. He pushes with the extended arm and throws his head, arm, and leg backwards and across his body. If he tucks the other arm and leg underneath him (the side to the roll), rolling over is much easier. Baby has really mastered rolling from tummy to back when he learns to keep one arm folded beneath him, thrusting out the other in full extension to push himself up and over. The elbow on that lower arm acts as a fulcrum and the whole arm as a sort of roll bar.

Most babies roll from tummy to back before rolling from back to tummy weeks or months later. In the prone position, baby can muster up more leverage with his arms and can roll better on the rounded contour of his abdomen. Rolling over seems to be a function of both baby's temperament and motor maturation. Very active babies tend to roll over earlier (at two to three months) whereas "easier" babies roll over around four to five months.

Why does your baby want to roll over? First, your baby wants to change his body position and explore new ways of moving. Another motivation for rolling over is that it facilitates reaching. Some babies learn to roll toward a desired toy long before they learn to crawl. Rolling toward a desired object is especially effective in encouraging baby to roll from back to stomach. Place a desired toy to the side of your baby above the level of his head and just beyond his comfortable reach. He will crane his neck around in order to see the desired toy as he pulls his torso into an arching position. He begins reaching with his shoulders by twisting the upper part of his torso sideways and then thrusts his twisting torso toward the enticing toy. When he lands on his tummy, baby can use this position to scoot and pivot toward the desired toy.

STANDING

Previously baby could stand only if you supported his trunk under his arms. Now he can bear almost all of his weight himself, his outstretched hands holding on only for balance.

LOCOMOTION

The increase in trunk and limb control enables baby to begin to get from place to place. If he is lying on a bed a few feet away from you when you both fall asleep, you may awaken a few hours later to find that he has squirmed and wiggled his way over to nestle up against you. By five months most babies are able to muster up just enough motor power with their arms and legs to worm their way a few feet across the bed or rug. True creeping and crawling usually do not begin until a few months later.

Social Communication

Enhanced visual acuity and more refined gesture skills make baby's needs and moods easier to read. Most of these needs fall into five categories:

"I want to be picked up and carried."
"I want to be put down."
"I'm bored."
"I'm tired."
"I'm hungry."

The cue that baby wants to be picked up and carried is the easiest to decode. He fusses, extends his

"I'm tired" signals

eyes, hands, and body toward you and quiets as soon as you pick him up. When he is being carried, your baby may occasionally surprise you by fussing and squirming in your arms and looking toward the floor. This is often a signal that he wants to be put down and left to kick and play freestyle on the floor. In the previous months most of baby's fussiness meant that he wanted to be picked up and carried. As his motor skills develop, the reverse may sometimes be true.

Even with the tremendous surge in visual-motor capabilities, five-month-old babies seem to get bored frequently. This tendency lessens when they can sit up by themselves. Signs that baby is bored include: a dull, lifeless stare, an expressionless face, and the beginning of fussing. If you catch this early and give him something interesting to look at, he will become happy again. But if he is not rescued from the doldrums, the fussing will progress into a full-fledged cry. Baby will then need to be picked up, carried, and stimulated with more than just something new to look at.

When baby is sending "I'm tired" signals, he continues to fuss after he is picked up. His crankiness escalates and new sights and surroundings do not seem to settle him. When you sit down, rock, or lie down and nurse him, he quiets.

The "I'm hungry signs" are unique sounds and gestures reserved for eating that may go something like this. Baby no longer begins the dinner call by crying. Instead, he lets out a string of short vowel sounds ("Ah-ah-ah") created by short bursts of inhaling and exhaling. He may also use breathy sounds, accompanied by nuzzling gestures as he orients himself toward the breast with his head and body and grabs or pulls with his hands.

Fun with Your Five-Month-Old

Play jumping jacks. Lie baby on his back across your lap with his feet planted against your waist. Pull him to the standing position holding on to his arms. You will notice his delight in being able to straighten out his back, board-like, as he is pulled completely up into the standing position, balancing with his feet on your lap. Baby then likes to bounce up and down on your lap as you securely hold on to both his hands or support him underneath his arms. Baby delights in being able to propel himself upward with his foot and leg power. If you get into the rhythm of this bouncing you can momentarily let him go as he drops down and then bounces up again under his own power. Baby also enjoys practicing back dives from this jumping jack position.

Hand play. Baby's reaching skills at this age make hand play a favorite. Babies like to clutch their clothing, blankets, your hair, your glasses, beaded necklaces, anything within reach. Any part of your body is fair game for reaching. Baby may grab a fistful of Daddy's chest hair. As you yell "ouch" baby squeals with delight at his achievement. Baby will now reach for and hold onto the bottle or breast during feeding, though only for a short time. Breastfeeding mothers may notice that babies begin to pat the breast throughout the feeding. Babies' increasing attention span may allow them to spend as long as ten to fifteen minutes in hand play, clutching their own hands, their own clothing, and various rattles and block-like objects within their grasp.

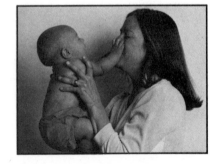

Besides playing with their own fingers, babies like to play with your fingers. If you hold your finger within his reaching distance baby will grab it with one or both hands and pull it into his mouth. Babies seem to enjoy their recently attained ability

Investigating a knot of yarn

to bring their environment and parts of other people in toward themselves. Capitalize on this by choosing appropriate toys: squeeze toys, squeak toys, toys of different shapes and textures, and toys that baby can really sink his hands into (such as a pile of yarn tied together—but don't leave him alone with this). When baby shows good reaching and grasping skills, cubes (wooden, rubber, or foam) are favorite toys for fun and learning.

Block play. Begin with small blocks of contrasting colors. Baby can easily grasp this size with his whole hand and truly feel that he has complete control of this object. Sit your baby in a high chair, propping him up with pillows until he is old enough to sit steadily in the chair unsupported. Place the blocks on the tray in front of baby and you can observe the amazing play skills of the five-month-old. Baby will grab a block in a mitten-like grasp and transfer it from hand to hand or from hand to lips. He will hold one block in one hand and grab a second block with the other. If you then place a third block in front of him, baby is encouraged to make a decision about what to do with the third block. Sometime around the fifth or sixth month baby will learn to put one block down to grab the other. Banging the blocks on the table, fondling them, and turning them over and over from hand to hand is a valuable play and learning exercise. Block play also helps to teach thumb and forefinger grasping, the mature form of grasping which develops over the next few months.

Safety tip

Toys such as blocks and balls should have a diameter of at least 1-3/8 inch so that baby can't swallow them.

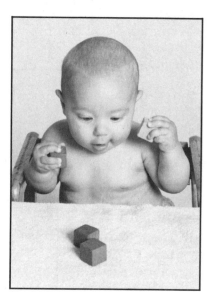

Block play: making decisions

Table fun. Baby enjoys sitting on your lap at the dinner table and playing with paper or cloth napkins and eating utensils. He may even show some interest in your food at this stage. Because of his quick darting reach, you need to be very careful to keep dangerous utensils, such as knives, and hot food and beverages well away from baby.

Mirror play. Holding your baby in front of a mirror allows him to flirt with his whole body. If you hold your baby during mirror play so that he can see both of your reflections, he can begin to understand that the baby he sees is himself.

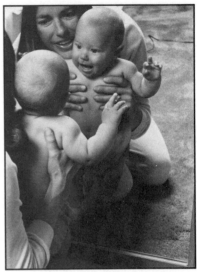

"If that's Mom, the baby must be me."

Cushion play. We have found that one of the most exciting and fun play activities beginning at five months is the use of homemade cylinder cushions and wedges. These pieces of foam can be obtained at an upholstery shop. Cylindrical foam shapes (bolsters) seven to ten inches in diameter and approximately two feet long make excellent rolling cushions for baby to practice trunk, head, and reaching exercises. It is also fun for parents to hold baby by the feet and play wheelbarrow. Wedge-shaped cushions are also fun for babies beginning in the fourth or fifth month. Wedges support babies' chests, allowing them to dangle their hands over the edge of the wedge and play with objects within their grasp. Use wedges three to four inches high for this age. Patterned covers with lots of contrast are the most appealing for babies. Babies also enjoy the mobility that these floor cushions allow. Drape baby over the cylindrical cushion and you will notice that he will push himself forward by digging his toes into the carpet and will learn to rock himself back and forth on the cushion using his own foot power.

Sofa sitting. The corner of the sofa is an ideal place to prop baby when he hasn't quite mastered sitting. He will enjoy viewing the living room from this grown-up vantage point. Don't leave him unattended in this position, though.

Holding patterns. Many mothers find that their babies are growing too large to be comfortable in a

Playing wheelbarrow

Infant sling for carrying baby on mother's hip

front carrier at this age and are more comfortable in hip carriers. Hip carriers place most of baby's weight on your hip rather than your shoulders. They also allow baby a greater range of motion with his head and facilitate eye-to-eye contact and parent-baby dialoguing.

Magic breath. A trick which is both fun for parents and comforting for baby is to breathe gently on baby's head. This often works to keep babies content in car seats, to prevent premature awakening, or simply to divert baby's attention during an accelerating fussy spell. Baby stops momentarily to enjoy this warm feeling and forgets why he was fussing.

SUMMARY: *FOUR TO FIVE MONTHS*

Large motor

- Pushes up on partially extended arms, chest and part of tummy off floor. Plays airplane: rocks on tummy, flaps arms and legs.
- Creeps and wiggles a few feet.
- Cranes neck forward to see and grab toes when lying on back.
- Holds entire weight on legs when supported standing.
- Assists by lifting head, flexing elbows when pulled to sit.
- Sits propped up with pillows or leaning forward on both hands; can lift one hand to reach for toy.

Fine motor

- One-handed, more precise reaching for toys within arm's length.
- Transfers objects purposefully from hand to hand, hand to mouth.
- Hand accommodates to shape of object before making contact.
- Grabs and plays with necklaces, glasses, hair.

Language/ social

- Babbling begins.
- Crying diminishes as expressive sounds and gestures increase.
- Attempts to mimic caregiver's sounds.
- Responds to labeling accompanied by directing gestures.
- Develops rhythmic dialogue, turn-taking.

Cognitive

- Tracks familiar person leaving room, pursues dropped toys.
- Attention span increases; may play with blocks and small toys ten to fifteen minutes.
- Interested in colors, small objects, picture books, squeeze-and-squeak toys, different textures.

CHAPTER
NINE:
THE
SIXTH
MONTH

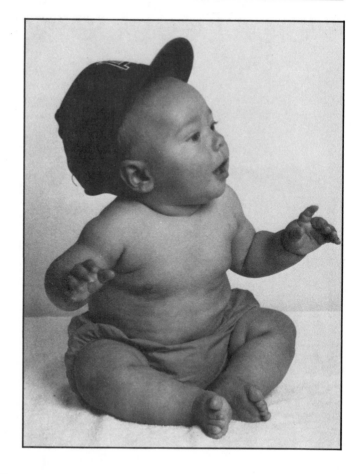

Sitting Up

Six-month-olds sit straight up and face the world head on. No longer are they confined to viewing their environment from the bottom up while lying on their backs. They can now spend most of their waking hours sitting unsupported, propped up on cushions, or placed in high chairs, viewing the world from a new, upright perspective.

One of the major developmental milestones for human babies is attaining a completely upright posture, in other words, standing. This is usually achieved around one year. By six months your baby is halfway there.

Motor Development

Learning how to sit is the highlight of motor development during the six-to-nine-month period. Because the spinal cord matures from head to bottom, baby can hold his upper back muscles straight before he can support his weight with the lower ones. Between the fourth and fifth months baby begins sitting momentarily, upper back straight and lower back slumped forward, propped up with one or both arms. He teeters a bit and then topples all the way forward or to the side. He gradually learns that he can stop a fall to the side by extending his hand. He also learns that he can momentarily lift one hand while balancing with the other hand.

SITTING ALONE

As the lower back muscles grow stronger between five and six months, baby momentarily sits with his back held straight but at a forty-five degree angle to the floor. He still must prop himself up with his hands. Around six months baby begins to let go with one hand and eventually, holding one or both hands out to the side for balance, straightens his lower back muscles and sits erect perpendicular to the floor. In the early stages of sitting alone, baby teeters and wobbles on his rounded bottom while thrusting out his arms for sideways balance. He brings his center of gravity forward, balancing over his legs which are flexed diamond-shaped in front of him. The six-month old soon learns that the most comfortable and secure way to sit is to bend slightly forward and use his legs as props.

Backwards and sideways falls are common for the beginning sitter because he does not have the strength or balance to right himself when he begins to topple to one side. Surround him with pillows when he is practicing sitting, because falling backward onto a hard surface may scare baby and

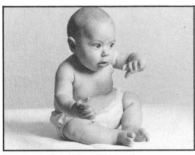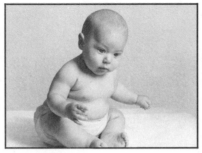

Balancing while sitting alone

dampen his motivation to perfect his sitting skills. You will notice that your beginning sitter uses his arms and legs to balance himself with his weight forward. This helps prevent backward falls. Toward the end of the six month most babies will develop the strength and quickness to react and right themselves if they have leaned too far forward or backward. A baby who can sit erect skillfully enough to use both hands for play and not for balance is truly siting alone. This occurs around six or seven months of age.

Early in the process of learning to sit baby keeps his arms and head mostly pointing straight ahead. This posture facilitates balance. As baby's balance improves he learns to rotate his head a full 180 degrees and use his arms to one side or the other without falling over. It is beautiful to watch the rhythm and balance of baby's arms and hands develop while he learns to sit and reach. At first, baby reaches to the side with one hand toward a toy and thrusts the other hand out for balance. As balance improves, baby can reach to the side with both hands without toppling over toward that side.

Helping your baby to enjoy sitting. To cushion the inevitable backwards and sideways falls, surround baby with pillows. A horseshoe-shaped piece of foam rubber helps to steady the wobbly beginning sitter. Hollowing out an area in the sand for baby's rounded bottom is another fun way of helping baby to enjoy sitting. Or you can sit him on the floor

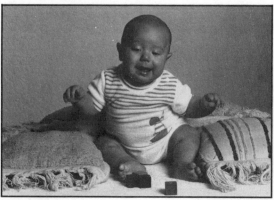

Pillows cushion the beginning sitter's tumbles.

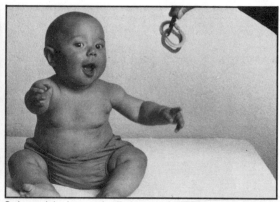

Being able to use both hands for play tests baby's sitting skills.

between your outstretched legs to help him balance safely. Place toys, such as blocks, in front of baby to motivate him to lift his hands from the floor. After baby masters picking up blocks in front of him, dangle a favorite toy at eye level to encourage him to sit erect and use his hands for play straight out in front of him. After this you can entice him to turn his head and arms to one side or the other to grab his toys.

Sitting unsupported is also a major milestone for parents. It brings relief from the demands of babies who previously wanted to be held all the time. For many babies sitting on the floor or in a high chair and playing with toys is a good solution to boredom. Sitting in the high chair also allows baby to take his place at the family table and enjoy and observe everyone else. The more creative and secure baby's sitting environment, the longer he will sit and play and the less he will fuss. At this stage baby does not yet have the motor skills or strength to assume the sitting position by himself. When the beginning sitter topples sideways or backwards, a quick cry of protest will summon his caregiver to quickly return him to the sitting position. As baby learns to right himself, these cries for help become less frequent. As baby begins to fall sideways and backwards less and less, he will learn to change his position by falling forward from a sit onto his tummy. With head up and arms outstretched he can continue his play without summoning a caregiver for help.

In the progression of learning motor skills baby's weight-bearing center moves downward from hands to elbows to hips to knees to feet. He goes from lying prone, to pushing up, to rocking on hands and knees, to crawling, and finally to pulling up to a standing position. Baby seems to progress an awkward notch every two to three months.

Pivoting. When lying on his tummy the six-month-old can push up on his extended arms to lift his chest off the ground almost as far as his belly button. All but the central part of his abdomen is off the floor; he rocks on his belly while kicking his legs and wiggling his arms and torso. He can pivot on his weighty abdomen, turning in a semi-circle to reach an enticing toy. Sometimes baby raises his outstretched arms off the floor in airplane fashion, teeter-totters on his tummy, and pivots around by the sheer momentum of his waving arms and legs.

The pivoting motion occasionally brings forward movement, as baby paddles with arms and legs, inching his abdomen across the floor. Sometimes baby will get frustrated after trying to drag his heavy tummy across the floor and will cry for help while changing position. Lunging forward may be baby's first act of locomotion from the sitting position; pivoting may be the start of moving from one spot to another while on his tummy.

Pushing up

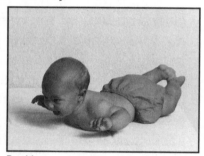

Rocking

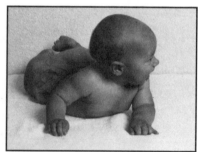

Pivoting

Propped on a foam rubber wedge

Another way that baby takes off from the prone push-up position is by rocking back and forth, a preliminary to crawling. When baby pushes up on his arms he occasionally tires and rests on his elbows. When baby's elbows are perpendicular to his trunk and the floor they serve as a fulcrum for his leaning and lurching forward. This leads into early crawling using the elbows and knees.

Some babies tire quickly in the push-up position and seem frustrated by having to use their arms for support and not for play. Placing a foam rubber wedge (about three inches thick) under baby's chest allows baby to play with toys in front of him at a more comfortable angle and for longer periods of time without getting exhausted. He can roll away from this position onto his back without hurting himself.

The combination of increasing motor skills and intense motivation allows baby to entertain himself when he is placed on his tummy on the floor with a toy just beyond his reach. He will dig in with his toes and fingers and squirm, scoot, or combat crawl toward his intended toy. He knows he can close that distance. Here's another floor game that babies enjoy: pull baby across the carpet by his heels so that he feels the texture rubbing his whole backside. Some babies this age can maintain a standing position if placed on their feet or allowed to lean against a piece of furniture such as a couch or the edge of a bathtub. Baby may stand there supporting and balancing himself for a few minutes before losing his balance and lowering himself to the ground by bending his knees. Baby enjoys the new way of seeing things from the standing position. You will notice that when your baby truly enjoys a newly acquired developmental skill, he will be very intense about practicing it and will protest vehemently if his practice is interrupted.

 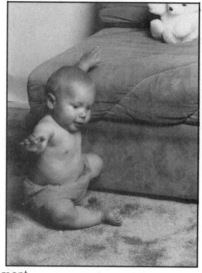

Leaning against the couch to stand—for a moment

PLAYPENS

Except in special situations, I generally discourage the use of playpens, especially for the infant six months or older who can pull himself up using the sides of the pen. Playpens can be restricting and frustrating to baby, who wants to move out and explore rather than sit and play. Babies this age can see across the room, and they want—perhaps need—to explore what they can see. Within reason and with appropriate safety precautions, consider the whole room and later, the whole house, as your baby's playpen.

Playpens have a limited use for protecting younger infants in special family situations or in a busy work place. Baby has his favorite toys within easy grabbing distance and can play safely and contentedly in a defined and familiar space.

HAND-EYE COORDINATION

Around six months baby's reaching and grasping motions become more one-handed, purposeful, and tenacious. He can quickly and consistently take a toy that you hand him. The ability to sit opens up new ways for baby to use his hands. Baby's attention span lengthens, allowing him to entertain himself and giving you a rest.

Reaching with both hands

Exploring with the eyes

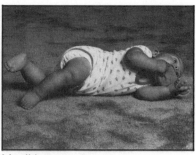

Mouthing

Watch how intently baby plays with a favorite toy. He does three main things with it. He explores the toy with his hands, brings it to his mouth, and examines it with his eyes. When baby is fingering the toy with his arms outstretched he is able to focus on the toy. As he draws it closer to his face in order to mouth it, his eyes try to keep a fix on the object, but he can't focus on it as it nears his mouth. So he stretches out his arms again to bring the object back to a comfortable focal distance. He repeats this hand-eye-mouth exploration over and over, vocalizing his delight in his new play skills.

Pointing. The way our six-month-old son Matthew began pointing at the family cat provides a good illustration of how babies begin touching and pointing at objects. Matthew approached the unsuspecting cat for the first time with his fingers extended, the index finger in the lead. He first touched the cat with just the tip of his index finger. He explored the cat for a while with the tips of all his fingers before resting his whole hand upon the cat and clutching the fur with his clenched fist. Babies begin pointing and touching in a way similar to how new mothers have been observed touching their babies for the first time, first with their fingertips and then with their fully opened hands. Some researchers feel that pointing is one of the earliest signs of communication.

Baby also begins to be able to understand your pointing at this age. When you point at an interesting object such as a pet or a ball baby begins to understand that you are referring to that thing and that you wish to engage baby in interaction with it.

Social-directing. Around six months baby begins to use his reach-out-and-touch-someone skills to signal his needs. He reaches up with arms and hands outstretched to say "Please pick me up." Besides using his own hands to signal a need, baby begins to direct your hands to move with his. He will grasp your finger and make your hand and arm move with him in energetic play. This activity is most noticeable during nursing.

Being able to reach for things stimulates baby to explore his body parts. He watches his toes go flying by in front of his eyes. He cranes his neck forward and bends his legs upward, bringing his toes within reach of his outstretched hands. As with so many other objects, once baby has a firm grasp of his toes he often brings them to his mouth. Notice that baby often points his big toe upward making it an easier target to grab.

Not only does baby like to grab and suck on his own body parts; he also frequently grabs at parts of you within his reach, such as your nose, hair, or glasses. A favorite game is sucking on your chin while stroking your face with his hands. During the early months you spent much time touching and grooming your baby. Now he can reach out and do the same to you.

Sucking on mom's chin

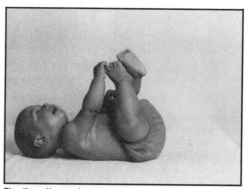
Finding those toes

Cognitive Development

In earlier stages of cognitive development, the mental schema the infant developed were primarily oriented at himself and at what gave him pleasure and comfort. The next stage is called the **sensorimotor period** because the infant now starts to direct his activities to the world outside himself through the use of his senses and his motor skills. The developing infant also becomes increasingly capable of clicking into more than one mental groove at a time which means he is able to combine his skills. Increasingly sophisticated hand skills and the beginnings of locomotion enable the infant to develop intentionality as well as decision-making and problem-solving skills.

For example, hand skills allow baby to pick up blocks of varying sizes, to pick up more than one block, to fit one block on top of another, to discover the many other different things he can do with the block (banging, stacking, dropping). The primary pattern of behavior (picking up the block) branches out into many associated patterns of behavior (the many things baby can do with the blocks once he has grabbed them). This leads to decision-making

Problem-solving during block play.

The newborn uses his hands to touch his face.

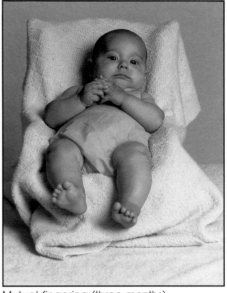
Mutual fingering (three months)

Batting at a mobile—more misses than hits at two months.

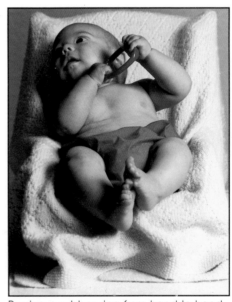
Passing a rubber ring from hand to hand (four months)

FINE MOTOR DEVELOPMENT

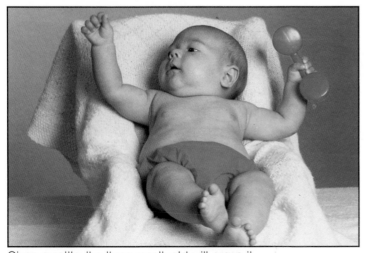
Given a rattle, the three-month-old will grasp it.

Grabbing for a fistful of block (five months)

Finger feeding (six months)

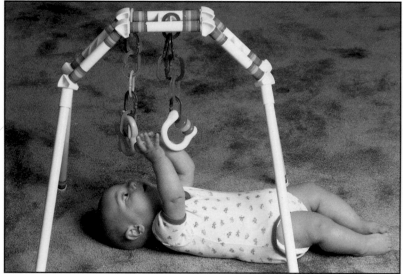

Reaching and gathering-in with both hands (six months)

Visually directed reaching (five months)

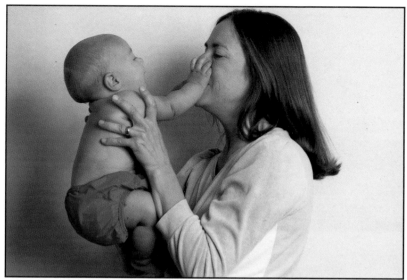

Exploring mother's face (six months)

Reaching for floating bubbles (eight months)

Pouncing on the ball (seven months)

REACHING AND GRABBING
SKILLS

Container play (ten months)

MATURE
MOTOR SKILLS

Using the thumb and fingers to grab some cereal (eight months)

Picking up a raisin in an elegant pincer grasp (eleven months)

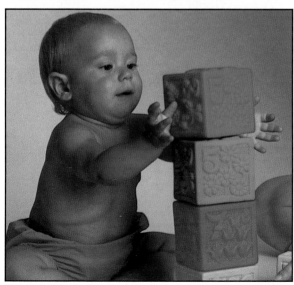

Stacking blocks (twelve months)

and also presents problems to solve—how can baby pick up a third block if he already has a block in each hand?

The possibility of locomotion fosters more problem-solving and decision-making. For example, baby sees a block across the room. He wants to reach the block. He must find a way to get to where he wants to go.

During this stage the brain centers for emotions also develop. This coupled with the baby's increasing realization that there are certain things he cannot do given his current physical abilities (find and recover a toy dropped from his high chair) inevitably lead to expressions of frustration. At the same time that these frustrations lead to behavior that may be difficult for parents to tolerate (whining, quick explosions of rage), the baby's ability to hold his caregivers' attention with more exciting play activities leads to emotional expressions that are more delightful, such as hilarious laughing.

Teething

From six months on so many new things happen so fast that parents often feel that babyhood is slipping away much too quickly. Teething often brings not only physical discomfort for baby but also these sorts of grieving emotions for parents. When you see the tooth pushing through baby's gums, you know the days of beautiful toothless grins are gone for good. You may look at his little gum line each day with apprehension to see whether the tooth is all that noticeable and then breathe a sigh of relief when you see that there really is very little to look at. But when the spoon he is chewing on makes that inevitable clinking sound, the tooth is there and there's no denying it.

Teething bothers most babies—and parents. The most common signs associated with teething are profuse drooling, often associated with a "drool rash" around mouth and cheeks; diminished appetite, irritability, slight fever, night-waking, and loose stools with a resulting diaper rash. Baby may temporarily lose interest in feeding or even stage a nursing strike during teething. When the drool collects in the back of baby's throat it may produce a raspy sound that is confused with a cold. But babies don't get runny noses with teething—a drippy nose is a cold! Treatment for teething discomfort consists of: pain relievers (check with your doctor), cold applied to the gums (a frozen banana or a cool teething ring works well), and massaging the gums.

The timing and sequence of teething is extremely variable. In most infants the two lower central incisors appear around six to seven months, followed by the two upper central incisors and the upper lateral incisors over the next few months. As a general guide baby will get one new tooth each month from six months to two years.

SUMMARY: *FIVE TO SIX MONTHS*

Large motor	• Lifts chest and almost all of tummy off floor, pushes up on extended arms; may pivot around in circle.
	• Rolls from back to tummy.
	• Sits erect briefly, uses hands for balance and to break sideways fall. May still slump slightly forward.
	• May stand momentarily, supported by furniture.
Fine motor	• One-handed reaching is more purposeful and tenacious.
	• Picks up two blocks, bangs them on table; may put one down to pick up a third.
	• Pointing is more noticeable.
	• Explores body parts with hands.
	• Uses whole hand to rake in and pick up small object.

• Longer strings of babbling noises.

• Produces greater variety of sounds using lip, mouth movements.

• Talks to toys, mirror image during play.

• Social directing: directs parent's hands toward himself; uses arms to signal needs.

Language/social

• Sitting allows longer play, more self-entertainment.

• More complex block play; appears to be making decisions.

• Stranger anxiety begins.

• May be interested in feeding self (very messy).

• Improved ability to imitate facial expressions.

Cognitive/play

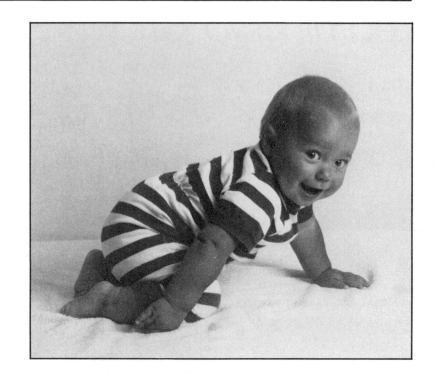

Moving Out

The period of babies' development between six and nine months is characterized by two main accomplishments: going from sitting to crawling and learning to pick up objects with the thumb and forefinger.

Sitting is a primary developmental skill which triggers a long series of additional accomplishments. By six to seven months most babies can sit unsupported and can rotate their heads and arms without toppling over. Their stronger lower back muscles enable them to right themselves. Since they no longer need their arms for balance they are able to use them more for socializing and for play. Baby now sees his environment straight on, a different perspective than the one he had lying on his back.

Learning to Crawl

Lengthening and lunging. Picture your six- to seven-month-old sitting in the middle of the room a few feet from various toys. His intense curiosity and desire to reach the toys, coupled with the increasing strength of trunk, arm, and leg muscles, seem to plant in his mind the idea, "I know I can get to those toys, but how?" The desire to move forward encourages baby to develop the skills of lengthening and lunging. It is fascinating to witness the gradual development of forward lunging as baby transforms his stationary skill—sitting—into a motor skill. This is the beginning stage of crawling.

At first, you will notice your baby bending forward to lengthen his reach, extending his hands and arms toward the desired toy and raking it in until it is comfortably within reach and can be manipulated with both hands. Next, baby learns to fold his legs toward himself, heels touching his diaper area. This tucked-in position shortens the rocking axis, allowing baby to roll forward over his feet. As baby begins lunging forward on his little rocker bottom, he builds up momentum until the forward lunging movements of his body gradually overcome his weight, and he completes the lunge, falling on his tummy just short of his objective.

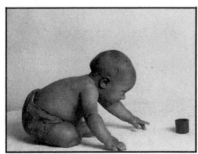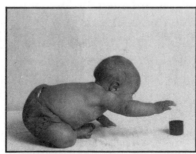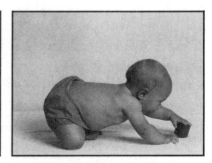

Lengthening and lunging: the beginning of crawling

Safety tip

When baby is learning these lunging forward skills use soft toys (cloth or rubber rather than wood or plastic). This will prevent injuries in case baby falls on top of the toy.

LOCOMOTION

The terms crawling and creeping are often used interchangeably or mean different things to different writers. Crawling refers to an early style of movement on bent knees and elbows. Creeping is a more advanced stage of crawling that begins around nine or ten months when baby's abdomen and hips are completely off the floor and he moves forward on hands and knees or hands and feet. Crawling usually precedes creeping by a couple of months. Because most people seldom use the term creeping to describe a baby's movements, I shall refer to all locomotion using arms and legs as crawling.

Baby's early attempts at locomotion on his tummy are ineffectual and frustrating. As is true for many developmental skills, intense desire precedes ability. His arms and legs kick and push in swimming movements that make him look like a stuck turtle. Baby's weighty abdomen just doesn't budge, despite the propelling forces of his arms and legs. Initially baby crawls with his hands and arms only, dragging his legs along behind him. Neurological development progresses from head to toe, so his upper extremities are capable of refined movement before the lower ones.

Pivoting is an early form of locomotion. When baby is able to hold his entire chest off the floor he learns to pivot on his tummy by criss-crossing his arms and turning his head and trunk in the direction he wishes to turn. His body turns in a circle, with the legs dragging behind his trunk.

The styles of the beginning crawler vary tremendously from baby to baby. Some babies will inchworm along the floor, keeping the whole body close

"Commando" crawling

to the surface. This turns into a commando-type crawl where baby squirms forward on his tucked-in elbows, his head scanning from side to side searching for objects to capture. Some babies will begin to move backwards rather than forwards, in a crab-like crawl, pushing rather than pulling with their arms. Other babies prefer to dig in with their feet, lifting their bodies off the ground between their extended legs and arms. They then thrust with their legs, propelling themselves forward in a leap-frog fashion a foot or two at a time.

A major turning point in mastering crawling skills comes when baby learns to use arms and legs together. He discovers that he can move most efficiently if his elbow and the opposite knee move at the same rate and the same time. He has found his "wheels" and is now ready to explore various ways to roll on them.

Cross crawling. The next refinement in baby's developing effective ground transportation is cross crawling. This means that the arm on one side and the leg on the opposite side come forward together. This allows baby to balance steadily on the hand and knee which remain in contact with the floor. This style of crawling is the most efficient and speedy, and the most likely to produce travel in a straight line. (You can test this out by getting down on the floor and trying it.) Cross crawling teaches baby to use one side of his body to balance the other. It is also a precursor to some of the balancing skills needed for walking.

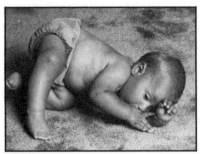

Bridging: elbows and knees to hands and feet

Bridging. As baby's crawling skills develop he gradually gets more and more of his trunk off the ground. He makes a "bridge" on elbows and knees, then hands and knees. He may even progress to bridging from hands to feet and "bear walking" just before he learns to walk upright.

Learning to crawl and eventually to walk is more than mastering getting from place to place. It is also an exercise in problem-solving. Imagine what is going on in the mind of the seven-month-old who is beginning to explore forward motion. He first learns to be aware of his moving parts—arms, hands, legs, feet. He also has an intense desire to learn about objects—toys or other things that may be lying just out of reach. He decides to use the motion to attain the objects and so, begins to experiment with various body movements—squirming, rolling, scooting—each time trying different combinations of all the movements he can make. He adopts the motions that are successful and eventually develops a rhythmic crawling style which helps him reach his goal. When a baby finds an efficient pattern of movement, this pattern clicks on an internal feeling of rightness.

Imagine all the elements of learning that are involved with mastering crawling. Baby experiments with various methods and then chooses the one which best serves his purpose. In so doing, he learns about problem-solving, cause-and-effect relationships ("Pushing with my feet makes me go this way"), and positive reinforcement ("Success at last! I think I'll try that again"). The more a baby experiences a better way of moving, the more motivated he is to continue practicing his skills.

One way you can observe the learning process is to place baby on different surfaces and watch how he accommodates his crawling motion to the different textures. When crawling on a deep pile carpet baby uses primarily his feet and toes to dig in, thrusting forward leap-frog style. On a smooth kitchen floor, baby is likely to inch-worm his way across in smaller increments because his trunk slides along more easily—if he has clothes on. Baby may prefer tiled surfaces because his hands and feet stick rather than slide, making it easier for him to pull and push his way across. It is amazing how baby learns to navigate using different styles on different "roads."

Baby likes to crawl up and over obstacles. Place a foam rubber roll or wedge between baby and an interesting toy. He will try lots of interesting maneuvers as he conquers this obstacle in relentless pursuit of his toy. Stairs are also an enticement at this stage. Baby crawls up a single step and down again, pausing frequently to assess his new ability.

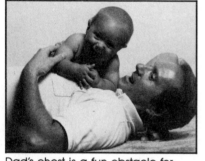

Dad's chest is a fun obstacle for beginning crawlers

GOING FROM CRAWLING TO SITTING

Babies enjoy combining all their new skills. Going from the crawling to the sitting position is one of the most fascinating maneuvers of this stage. Around seven months baby can go from sitting to lunging forward and then to crawling. Baby next learns how to maneuver his body in the opposite sequence, going from the crawling position back to a full sit. You may notice that your baby fusses out of frustration when trying to go from the crawling to the sitting position, but he will gradually learn to change positions faster, more skillfully, and with less fuss.

Going from sitting to crawling

To master this maneuver baby uses the foot tuck, similar to the skill he used in lunging forward from sitting to crawling. Baby is crawling along and then quickly stops, tucks one foot underneath, and swings sideways, vaulting over the tucked-in foot while digging in and pushing with the other foot and hands. And there he is, sitting upright. This ability is another milestone of relief for parents. The beginning sitter needed a helper nearby, but no more.

PULLING TO STAND

The intense desire to ascend from the horizontal to vertical position stimulates baby to grab hold of furniture and railings and pull himself up to a standing position. Baby expresses great delight in his newly found skill of pulling up.

Standing supported. When babies reach the pulling-up stage, they have enough strength to keep their legs, hips, and trunk straight while standing briefly, holding your hands for balance. At this age baby is also able to stand leaning against a sofa for five to ten minutes, but if he tries to turn towards you, he will lose his balance and crumple to the floor. Many babies at this stage still do not plant their whole foot on the floor, preferring to stand on tiptoe with their feet turned in, a position which greatly compromises their balance. The tip-toe tendency is probably due to baby tensing his whole body to get into this exciting new position. When baby is able to stand flat-footed and straight-legged, he will

Standing on tiptoe

stand for a longer time, holding on only for balance. If baby is standing hanging onto a sofa and his feet are turned in and overlapping, gently turn them out and plant them flat, teaching him to use his feet as a firm base of support. If baby still crumples easily when standing, support his bending legs with your hands around the back of his knees. By taking some of the frustrations out of failed attempts, you can help baby enjoy a new skill and thereby enhance its development.

What about walkers? It is vitally important that babies learn to use their body parts in the normal progression that they were designed to work. I do not advise parents to use walkers or any other devices which encourage babies to rely on outside assistance for locomotion rather than on their own creativity or initiative. I believe that babies are designed to progress from sitting to standing to walking by experimenting with their own body parts and not with the aid of wheels or devices. In all but the most impulsive infants, mental and motor abilities develop in parallel. A baby's ability to think through a situation prevents him from using his newly found motor skills in situations he is not yet able to handle. Walkers give babies motor skills that will get them into situations that they are not yet able to cope with mentally. This produces accidents. In general, walkers are unsafe and possibly may be detrimental to baby's natural motor development. Most babies, however, enjoy walkers. A few minutes of supervised play is probably all right; spending a lot of time in a walker is not advisable.

CRUISING

Around eight to nine months of age, babies lean against furniture only for balance, but are able to bear their own weight entirely. They begin to cruise around, taking small steps while holding on to walls and furniture for balance. Next comes letting go: first baby lets go with one hand and turns sideways from the furniture, still leaning on it for a bit of support. Periodically baby tries letting go with both hands and may even stand by himself for a few moments before falling or grabbing onto the nearby couch or table.

Baby can use his stronger limb and trunk muscles to protect himself from falls as well as to move. These righting movements are most noticeable when baby falls sideways or backwards. When the sitting-up baby leans too far to one side and senses he's going to fall he places his arm down on the ground to brace himself. To right himself when falling backward, the baby who is rocking back and forth on his bottom straightens out his legs in front of him to counterbalance the backward fall. Even if baby does fall backwards he is able to tense his trunk muscles enough to save his head from hitting the floor. The baby controls the rate of descent so that he goes over more slowly and softly. During this stage of development it is not so important how baby moves. The important thing is that he realizes his capability of moving from place to place and experiments with various ways of doing so. Sometimes he may dig in and scoot, other times he may twist and roll or even crawl. During the next stage of development he refines these various modes of transportation and selects the one which is most efficient.

Reinforcing motor skills. Each time our son Matthew learned a new skill, he seemed to do best amid the encouraging cheers of his siblings. Watch how your baby beams after accomplishing a new feat. As you notice his amazement and pleasure with himself, praise him: "Good, Matthew rolled over!" Also encourage near-misses and failures. When you acknowledge his performance, you encourage him to give an encore and to try again.

Hand Skills

The time from six to nine months is the pick-up-and-play stage. Baby's fascination for small objects complements his new locomotor skills. He will squirm around like a crab on the carpet to get at and pounce on scraps of paper or lint. Babies this age are like little carpet sweepers, picking up even the tiniest specks of dirt that are lying around. Parents should be especially vigilant about not leaving small mouthable objects lying within baby's grasp. Anything smaller than an inch and a half in diameter can be swallowed and should not be allowed near a baby. Babies delight in mouthing paper, and you will spend a lot of time retrieving soggy wads from baby's mouth. Notice that your baby likes to pick out small details such as the tip of a red push-pin stuck high up on the wall or a blob of red paint on a picture which he stares at and may even make attempts to pick up. Baby's fascination with small objects is especially noticeable when he sits on a sidewalk and stares at the ants crawling back and forth.

DEVELOPMENT OF THE PINCER GRASP

At the same time that baby's fascination for small objects develops, he also develops the capability to explore them by picking them up between the thumb and forefinger. Before this time, baby raked in objects and grabbed them with his whole hand, mitten-like, between his fingers and his palm. But now he begins to make pincer-like pick-ups using the thumb and the first two fingers.

The pincer grasp begins to develop around five or six months when baby begins to hold small objects between the first two fingers and the fatty area at the base of his thumb. Around seven or eight months baby begins to use the thumb along with

Raking-in

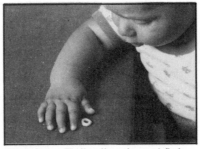
Grasping with the thumb and first two fingers

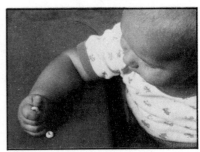
Thumb and forefinger grasp

the first two fingers. He progresses into a thumb and forefinger pincer grasp around eight or nine months, and thereafter refines it still further until he uses only the tips of his thumb and forefinger. Month by month, the development process is simply a matter of gradually working the object from the base of the palm, up the thumb, eventually to the tips of the finger and thumb.

In the early stages of developing the pincer grasp, baby makes frustrating and usually unsuccessful attempts to pick up small objects such as particles of food. At this age he can't quite get the thumb and forefinger to operate independently; the other fingers always seem to get in the way. Learning to get them out of the way of his thumb and forefinger is a major accomplishment.

Also, in the early stages he is not able to get his thumb and forefinger to work together. But he is still very interested in small objects, so he may rake a pile of Cheerios along the surface of a table to the edge and then try to scoop them into his chubby little hands. His raking is still paw-like, fingers outstretched, and involves his whole arm. After baby has raked an object toward himself, he may become frustrated at not being unable to pick it up. He will try various whole-handed maneuvers including pressing the object between both hands. This may really frustrate him because he thinks the object is lost when really, it's only buried somewhere in his pudgy little hands. As baby's picking-up ability matures you will notice that he uses less paw-like raking and more direct thumb and forefinger pick-ups.

Pointing is an early sign that baby is about to use the pincer grasp. Baby tucks his three fingers into his palm and points to something with the index finger. He touches the object with the pointed finger and soon the thumb follows the lead of the index finger and the pincer pick-up results.

BLOCK PLAY

Baby's ability to pick things up is most noticeable when he plays with blocks placed in front of him. Try this interesting exercise with blocks: put baby's blocks on a placemat just beyond his reach. He will lunge toward the blocks and realize they are out of his reach. After a brief show of frustration baby may grab and pull the placemat toward himself and voila! the blocks come toward him also. This becomes a great learning experience; baby can use one object to get another object.

Block play also helps baby learn about making decisions. Put three blocks in front of baby. He will grab and mouth one, then the other, and then attend to the third as if trying to decide how to get it. He may drop one of the blocks in his hands and grab the third one, or he may keep a tight hold on both blocks while raking in the third with his fists. Baby will bang two blocks together at this stage but makes no attempt to pile one block on the other. This skill matures several months later.

Babies love to pounce. When sitting, they hold their hands open, star-like, ready to pounce on anything in their reach, and their reaching becomes more direct and purposeful. Their hands are usually in the ready-to-pounce position, open wide, fingers extended, and are drawn toward any interesting object within reach. Babies show increasingly quick responses at this stage, especially if you slowly pull a block-carrying placemat across their path. Baby pounces on the block, grabs it with his whole hand or rakes it toward himself for closer observation.

Pouncing as the blocks go by

The hands of the six-to-nine-month-old usually need to be filled with something. When held in front of you your baby will grab your hair, glasses, nose, shirt, or blouse. He'll be especially attracted to strings or bows attached to your apparel. Baby will also notice and finger the snaps on his own clothing. (Buttons are potentially dangerous on baby's clothes because they can be pulled off and mouthed.) So intense is baby's desire to reach, grab and pick up that it is not wise to show him anything that he is not allowed to touch.

Nature provides ample targets for inquisitive little hands. To help baby develop his thumb and forefinger grasp try this simple exercise. Sit baby down in the grass. At first he will grab a whole clump of grass with his entire hand. Gradually he will become fascinated with the blades extending upward toward him and he will try to grasp individual pieces of grass with the thumb and the first two fingers. By repetitive trials he eventually learns that the thumb and forefinger pincer grasp is the best method for picking up one blade of grass at a time.

LEARNING TO RELEASE

An important part of baby's learning is developing the ability to release the grasped object. Babies become fascinated when an object they are holding, such as a piece of paper, floats slowly to the floor when they open their hands. Purposely releasing the object and watching it fall delights the curious baby. This leads to one of baby's favorite games, dropping. Baby now has the visual tracking ability to turn, notice, and follow a dropping object, but he soon tires and forgets the object. He may also take delight in dropping objects from his high chair and then watching you pick them up. Baby will soon associate the action of dropping with your reaction of leaning over and picking the object up. He learns to associate cause and effect.

Releasing also helps baby learn to transfer objects from hand to hand. When he did this earlier, it was mostly by accident. Now it becomes intentional. Complex mental processes must be going on during the simple act of transferring a ring from one hand to the other. Earlier baby held the ring with both hands and played a sort of tug of war. If one hand let go first, the other got the ring, and baby's eyes went from the empty hand to the hand that held the ring. This transferring is unintentional and jerky. Around six months baby seems to know when to let go. He releases the holding hand simultaneously with the pull of the free hand, resulting in a smooth, intentional transfer of the ring from one hand to the other. The ability to transfer toys extends baby's play time. He can sit and entertain himself for ten to twenty minutes, shuffling an object back and forth from one hand to the other. The combination of two skills, sitting without support and transferring objects, allows this shuffle play to happen.

GRABBING AND REACHING

The six-to-nine-month-old is more tenacious in his grasp. If you try to take something away from him, he resists your pull with a strong grasp of his fingers and a flexed arm. If you do manage to extract baby's favorite toy from his hands and put it on the floor in front of him, he will show an interest in it immediately and purposefully pounce on it, recapturing it in the grasp of both hands.

Baby also reaches more accurately at this stage. His reach is more direct, less hesitating and jerky, and he seldom overshoots the mark. Another fascinating milestone in the reach-grasp development is how baby accommodates his hands to the shape of the object. In the previous stage, baby would strike and palm the object, and his whole hand would encompass it, adjusting to its shape only after he touched it. Now, he begins to change his hand to fit the shape of the object before he actually reaches it. He has developed a visual "feel" for the object which helps him determine its shape before he touches it. Because the six-month-old has such a capability for quick strikes, it is difficult to fully appreciate the in-flight corrections that occur as his searching hands approach the target. Slow-motion videotapes show how baby's reaching hand begins to mold to the shape of the intended object even before touching it.

HAND DOMINANCE

Between six and nine months of age, parents may get a clue as to which is baby's dominant hand. If you put a toy in front of baby's midline he may quickly go for it with his dominant hand. If baby seems to be right-handed and you put a toy next to him on his left side, he may reach across his body with his right hand. His left hand stands in readiness to assist the right, but the right hand is the one that is doing the reaching.

Social Interaction

Baby's desire to play with objects on the floor may at times overcome his desire to be held. If a baby sees a desired object lying on the floor he will often zero in on that object with his eyes, dart his hands outward, and squirm from your arms until you put him down to pursue his intended prey. Babies become less interested in being in your arms and will often entertain themselves by sitting and playing with toys or crawling around the floor. For many babies this is the first time when they can truly entertain themselves.

Baby's inquisitive little hands are constantly darting out into the food you are eating, the newspaper you are reading, and the dangling apparel you are wearing. This activity is very noticeable when baby sits on your lap at the dinner table. Within a few seconds baby may rev up into a frenzy of grabbing activity that makes an absolute mess of plates, utensils, napkins, and anything else that gets in the way of his waving arms.

Besides using his hands and arms for play and movement, baby begins to realize that his arms and hands can be used to signal his caregivers. Instead of crying to be picked up baby will often look up with big eyes and extend his outstretched arms and hands toward you in a "please-pick-me-up" gesture. These gestures should be attended to as if baby were crying to you with his voice. Promptly responding to baby's hand signals, as you did to his crying signals, reinforces his use of body language as a means of communication.

The increasing use of his hands and fingers for social gesturing is especially noticeable in the way baby pats and strokes a familiar object such as your face or the family cat. It's beautiful to watch how baby uses his hands to reach out and pick up the things he wants and touch the people he loves.

SEPARATION ANXIETY

The development of new skills usually brings out interesting behaviors associated with these skills. This is most evident in the separation anxiety which most babies show around seven to eight months. Your baby may protest vehemently when you leave his sight for even a few minutes. I developed my own theory about separation anxiety as I watched

Matthew crawl across the room. Every five feet or so he would turn his head and check to see if Mom and Dad were there. Matthew at this age would often cry if he did not find us or if he saw us walking out of the room. Separation anxiety seems to begin when baby develops the locomotor skills needed to move away from his parents. Although he now has the power to initiate a separation, he is very fearful of it. Could it be that separation anxiety keeps baby from drifting beyond the parents' protective influence and that it has survival benefits?

A wise parent will respect a baby's separation anxiety. Continuous voice contact with an out-of-sight parent helps to alleviate separation anxiety. Most babies of seven or eight months have not yet developed object permanence; this means that if they cannot see or hear you, they think that you no longer exist. Object permanence usually does not develop until a later stage when baby develops sufficient memory to realize that you can continue to exist out of his sight. Even if you are in another room, periodically call out baby's name and reassure him that "Mommy's here." One day I watched

mama's coming

Matthew through a crack in the bathroom door after I had walked away and left him. He had watched me leave and continued to gaze at the space where he had last seen me, wondering and expecting me to reappear. Without waiting for Matthew to cry anxiously, I reassured him with the sound of my voice. As soon as he heard me speak he resumed his play, as if he realized he no longer had to worry about my disappearance.

The separation anxiety that is so characteristic of this stage suggests an important concept about weaning: the infant should separate from the mother and not the mother from the baby. The infant will not separate from the mother completely until he has the cognitive ability to develop a mental image of the mother and, as it were, take the mother with him. Locomotor and mental capabilities develop together and are mutually dependent on each other. They work together beautifully to promote a gradual weaning, as long as the caregiving environment creates the conditions which allow them to complement and not frustrate each other.

Researchers have used the term **hatching** for this process of baby's going from a sense of oneness with mother to the knowledge of his separateness. But while hatching implies a physical separation from the mother, cognitive development allows the baby not only to move away from the mother but also to move closer to her. This closeness is maintained by the ability to form mental images of the mother, an ability that matures in the last part of baby's first year.

STRANGER ANXIETY

Some babies develop stranger anxiety between six and nine months. Some very sensitive babies show signs of it already at four months. Others are not fearful of strangers until toddlerhood. Typically, baby will cling to you, look fearful, or even cry

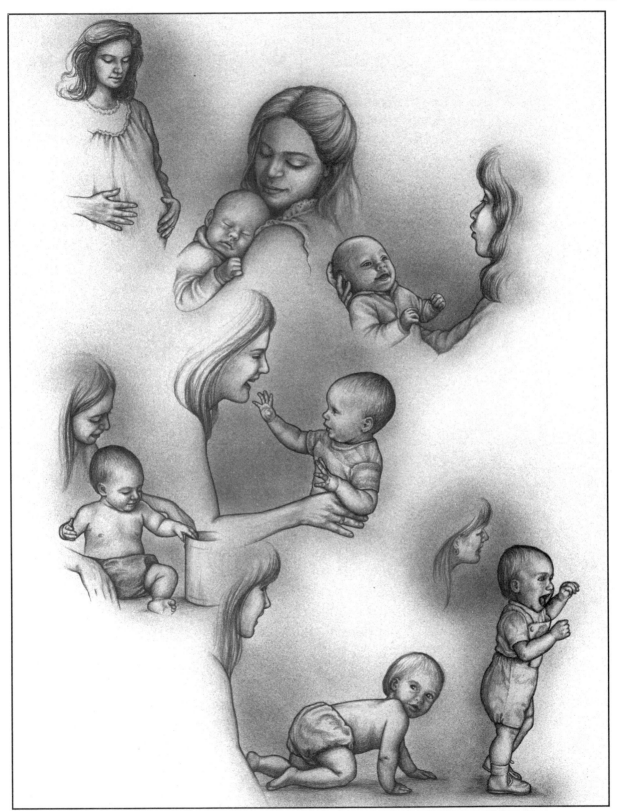

From oneness to separateness in the first year

when someone unfamiliar to him approaches. This reaction can be minimized if you quickly greet the approaching stranger while still some distance away. Then, still keeping some distance from the stranger, continue the joyful dialogue with a welcoming smile. (Moving gradually from the familiar to the unfamiliar is an important strategy at this age.) Your baby begins to form a concept about the stranger based on your reaction. If the stranger is okay with you, he or she is okay with baby. Babies use their parents as a standard against which to evaluate all others.

Warn significant "strangers" (grandparents, good friends) not to be too socially aggressive with your baby, but to let you set the stage so that eventually, baby will come to them. Or suggest they play with one of baby's favorite toys or an unfamiliar toy that will engage baby's interest. This may help your baby warm up to a stranger who, incidentally, possesses the toy he wants.

Language Development

In the first six months baby became comfortable producing sounds, exhibiting body language, and learning that these early cues mean something and would receive responses. During the next stage baby refines these sounds and body language into verbal and more advanced social communication.

BABBLING

Babbling, long repetitive strings of syllables consisting of consonants paired with vowels (for example, "Ba-ba," "Da-da," etc.), is a major language milestone that occurs around six months. Babbling sounds encompass the common speech sounds used in all the various languages of the world. They are the building blocks from which all future speech develops. Babies enjoy babbling. They begin to recognize a relationship between the way they shape their mouth and tongue and the sounds they produce. For example, "Ba-ba-ba" is made with the lips. Baby can change the sound to "Da-da-da" by using his tongue rather than his lips. Babies love to practice these newly produced sounds and may vocalize over and over for minutes. They also enjoy the reaction these sounds elicit in their audience. Babbling is often called baby's first speech.

Research comparing deaf infants to hearing infants has revealed a lot about the importance of the babbling stage. Having an awareness of his own sounds is necessary for a baby's proper speech development. Prior to six months there seems to be very little difference between the sounds produced by deaf and hearing infants. This suggests that during the first six months babies do not have to hear their own sounds in order to develop the ability to vocalize. However, after eight months there is a noticeable difference between hearing and deaf infants. Specifically, babbling in syllables may be absent in deaf infants.

Studies comparing the vocalization of babies raised in different language environments do not show that infants vocalize exactly alike, but infants do show a general similarity in vocal patterns across cultures, especially in babbling. Babies of different cultures seem to have a universal repertoire of sounds up until the age they start producing true words. Beginning around nine months babies begin to adapt these universal babbling sounds to the specific language of their culture, by learning to match the sounds they hear in response to the reinforcement and imitation they receive from their audience.

Around eight months babbling takes on a more communicative quality. Some "sentences" begin to sound like statements, others like questions. After practicing the sound over and over again babies

Imitating baby's babbling enhances language development.

eventually remember how to make the sound. They even seem to be thinking about what they are going to say. Specific sounds become associated with specific activities. These babbling sounds are very close to baby's first meaningful words. When associated with the gestures he makes, his sounds will help you understand what he is trying to tell you. Because parents are used to using both the sounds and the accompanying gestures to decode what baby means, they can usually understand what baby is saying at this stage, although strangers cannot. True words come later, when specific sounds are used for specific objects or actions.

Imitate baby's babbling and other body language. You can enhance your baby's babbling abilities by looking him in the eyes and echoing back his sounds. This reinforces baby's language skills and his desire to turn the babbling into true words.

Parents may notice that their baby occasionally shows brief periods where he doesn't seem to vocalize much. This curious phenomenon occurs when baby devotes a lot of energy and attention to developing another major skill such as crawling. Some babies seem to put development of one skill on hold when focusing on another.

BABY LANGUAGE

Between six and nine months babies become more sensitive to the intonations and inflections in your speech. They become more interested in how people speak rather than in what they say. Perceiving that a person's language is a reflection of inner feelings may be baby's first realization that speech is an emotional skill. As baby begins to read your feelings from the sounds and gestures of your language his own cues also become more readable.

Entry greetings. Babies develop specific social gestures in order to initiate a pleasing social interaction. For example, when daddy walks into the room baby's face lights up with a big smile as he turns toward daddy with his whole body and an expression on his face that says "Let's play."

Mood sounds. The universal "n" sound emerges at this stage to express babies' negative feelings. For example, when baby has had enough nursing but is still unhappy or is tired but doesn't want to go to sleep, he will vocalize a string of "Na-na-na." This will crescendo until it becomes more of a cry. In the beginning it is definitely vocalization and not crying, as if baby is using words to communicate to you that he is unhappy. Watch baby's face as he vocalizes the "na" sounds. The distress that he's feeling makes his eyes droop and look sad. His facial muscles are all pulled downward, and his mouth is twisted into an unhappy grimace, but he does not yet show the usual facial distortion that accompanies crying. Baby is definitely expressing himself vocally and facially without resorting to crying.

When baby is happy he tends to vocalize with a string of more happy sounds and excited playful gestures. Baby's facial configuration also reflects his playful mood. His eyes are bright and all his facial muscles are drawn upward. His cheeks bulge out with a smile, and he bounces his whole body in anticipation of play, all the time muttering joyful sounds such as "Um-um-um," "Ba-ba-ba," or "Uh-uh-uh." When baby needs to be comforted or wants to be held but is not distressed, he may vocalize with "Mum-mum-mum" and may even manage an occasional "Mama" or Dada."

Some babies sing their babbling noises when they are engrossed in play. They use one pitch for the first syllable and a new pitch for the next and then string out these various syllables and notes throughout the play activity. Sometimes baby can reflect a mood or a feeling by the way he stops vocalizing. This is especially true when baby expresses relief or discomfort. When you apply smooth ointment onto baby's sore bottom, he shows that he enjoys the feeling by becoming very quiet and wide-eyed, as if concentrating on the experience of feeling the ointment being smoothed onto those sensitive areas.

Because baby's language becomes more understandable at this stage, parents often find that their response time to baby's fussiness can lengthen a bit. During play, baby's fussing is sometimes goal-directed, a way of verbalizing his frustration while he works hard at reaching a goal (such as a nearby toy under a table) by himself without help.

Parents learn to discern when they should help and when they should stand back and watch baby achieve his goal, even if it means listening to his fussing for a bit. There is a point at which baby's fussiness is no longer constructive and he really needs your assistance to reach his goal.

RESPONDING TO LANGUAGE

Cue words are words or phrases spoken by the parents which trigger a consistent and predictable response from the baby. An example of this social cuing is the "Bump Heads Game" that I play with Matthew. I say, "Bump heads!" and Matthew and I gently bump foreheads. After repeating this game a number of times, Matthew takes the cue and actually starts moving toward me as I say the word "bump," even before I start moving toward him. His eyes suddenly twinkle and then close, his chin reaches forward for mine, and his whole body wiggles in closer to me as his head moves in for the bump. Matthew has recorded this game in his memory. When hearing the cue word "bump" he drops the needle in the right groove and sets the whole record playing. Even after weeks have passed without playing the game, baby is likely to respond to the same cue word when it is accompanied by the correct gestures and setting. This usually depends on how frequently the game has been played. Sometimes babies do seem to forget what the cue word means.

Word games are especially valuable for encouraging language and early memory. One that our babies have enjoyed goes like this:

Round and round the garden goes the teddy bear,
(Draw a circle around baby's tummy with your finger)
One step, two steps,
(Walk your fingers from his belly button to his neck)
Tickle you under there!
(Tickle him under the chin.)

When I start this game in an exaggerated, lilting sort of voice, Matthew very quickly recognizes that these words are an invitation to play and the beginning of fun.

As your baby matures, you will notice that he responds to cue words more consistently, even lifting his shirt for the "Teddy Bear" game. This is primarily due to his steadily improving memory.

Association. During this stage baby begins to associate words with objects in his environment. For example, one day I was showing eight-month-old Matthew a book with pictures of cats and said to him, "See the cat." He immediately looked up and away from the book and moved his head around in a purposeful way, trying to locate our family cat that I was telling him to look at. The noun cat had no meaning at all to him in terms of pictures in a book. To him, cat meant a furry thing that walked around the house. Baby becomes more proficient at associating words with things if his caregivers have consistently practiced the speech-enriching technique of labeling with him.

Dinner conversations. Baby's lengthening attention span and improving ability to sit up help him to stay in his high chair longer at the dinner table and to actually take part in the family conversation. When the conversation goes back and forth between one person and another, baby will focus on the person who is speaking. He will follow the conversation back and forth from person to person as he develops the important social language skill of listening. He has an interested look on his face and is definitely aware that a social exchange is going on between speakers. He is interested in it and perhaps wants to be a part of that exchange. Baby even begins to exchange glances with the family members around him.

Dancing. As baby's listening skills and attention span steadily improve, you may notice that he begins to wiggle his body, or dance, when he hears music. When you turn the music off, his dancing stops. When you turn it back on he resumes dancing.

Toys and Games

Toys and activities which complement the two new developmental skills of this stage, sitting up and picking up, will hold the six-to-nine-month-old baby's attention the longest.

Babies this age really like to get into things such as rustling paper. Reading a magazine uninterruptedly with baby on your lap is no longer possible. Baby lunges toward the magazine, crumples it in his hands, and draws it to his face in intense delight. If you wish to complete your reading, you'll have to give baby a substitute paper to play with. Use paper that makes a noise, the crinklier the better. Sit-and-pick-up activities are fun, especially when baby is surrounded by a smorgasbord of toys. In general, it is wise to give baby only a few toys at a time, but occasionally he will enjoy sitting in the middle of a pile of objects and making choice after choice.

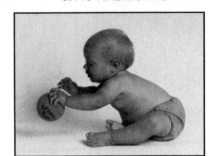

Mirror play. Now that baby can sit up unsupported, he likes to be placed within touching distance of a mirror. He can match his hands and face to the image in the mirror.

Grab balls. Balls and blocks are time-honored favorite toys of babies. While babies are too young to catch and throw at this stage, they can grab and hold a ball. Use balls that are large enough to be held with both hands, preferably made of cloth or soft foam that baby can get his fingers into and hold onto with one hand. You can help your baby discover the concept that a ball is for holding, throwing, and passing between two players. This awareness sets the stage for real ball play which begins in the next stage.

Playing on **foam bolsters** becomes even more fun at this stage because baby can now use these cushions to entertain himself. Drape him over the bolster cushion and place a toy just beyond his reach. Notice how baby digs his feet in, pushing himself forward and rolling on the foam cylinder in hot pursuit of the toy.

The **pick-pocket game** becomes a favorite at this stage. I noticed that when I held Matthew he

Pick-pocket game

immediately zeroed in on the pen protruding from my shirt pocket. He would pick it up with a precise grasp and hold it very possessively, not wishing to give it back. Babies learn to anticipate these activities and expect dad to wear his shirt with a pen in it. One time I came home from work wearing the same shirt and picked Matthew up. He reached toward my pocket, but to his surprise it was empty. He looked surprised and very disappointed.

The six-to-nine-month-old can be a lot of fun to play with. His skill at sitting, his attempts at locomotion, his new hand skills, and his language abilities bring greater variety to his activities. His desire to learn and refine these skills keeps him very busy. Instead of entertaining your baby, you may discover that he's entertaining you.

SUMMARY: *SIX TO NINE MONTHS*

Large motor

- Sits unsupported; lunges forward from sitting position.
- Crawling begins: crawls on belly first, then on hands and knees. Learns cross-crawling.
- Goes from sitting to crawling and back to sitting.
- Pulls self to standing; balances on tiptoe, feet turned in, holding onto furniture; pivots around in complete circle.
- Cruises while holding onto furniture.

Fine motor

- Pointing with index finger leads to more precise reaching.
- Pincer grasp develops; tries to pick up tiny objects.
- Pounces on moving toys.
- Releases toys and watches them fall.

Language/ social

- Greater variety in babbling.
- Combines sounds and gestures to express needs, emotions; body language is clearer.
- Becomes sensitive to inflections in parent's speech.
- Cue words from parents elicit predictable response; responds to own name.
- "N" sounds (as in "no") begin.
- May occasionally use "ma-ma" or "da-da" to refer to parent.

*Cognitive/
play*

• Stranger and separation anxieties begin.

• Enjoys word games; associates words with objects.

• Dances, wiggles body to music.

• Plays with mirror image.

• Enjoys peek-a-boo, pat-a-cake, block play, crumply paper, balls.

• Can sit and play for longer periods of time.

Moving Up

The most exciting development of the last quarter of
your baby's first year is the progression from crawling to walking. During these three months your
baby will also refine his hand-eye skills and will
prepare to utter his first real words. His memory
will improve and so will his ability to communicate.
By the end of the first year, your baby is well on
the way to being a toddler.

Locomotor Development

By nine months most babies have mastered a style of crawling that is efficient, comfortable, and speedy and that feels right to them. For most babies this means cross crawling. In order to appreciate its efficiency, you might want to experiment with it yourself. Notice that if you move the arm and leg on one side of your body at the same time you are momentarily off balance. Cross crawling—using opposing arms and legs—allows better balance. One limb from each side is on the floor at all times. If you were to watch a slow-motion videotape of baby's crawling you would notice that the hand on one side of the body moves forward just moments before the leg on the opposite side follows. Cross crawling prepares baby for many other physical skills. Efficient ways of walking, running, and throwing a ball all require the use of arms and legs in opposition to one another in order to provide balance. I don't believe cross crawling is an innate skill. It is a learned style. Practicing cross crawling will aid baby's coordination later on.

What about the baby who doesn't crawl much? Some specialists feel that a baby who does not crawl is at risk for problems later on. While this may be true of some babies, there are some perfectly normal, well-coordinated children who quickly by-pass the crawling stage to move on to other modes of locomotion. Two of our six children had a very short crawling stage. One scooted on his bottom with one leg straight out and the other leg bent under him. Our daughter Erin, at nine months, stopped crawling and "walked" on her knees. (Parental reinforcement influences locomotor styles. We thought both of these styles were so cute that we acted like cheerleaders.)

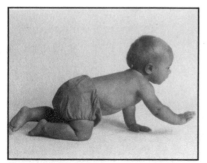

Cross-crawling

The mastery of a skill increases the baby's enjoyment and desire to experiment. You will notice that as your baby settles into a comfortable crawling style his speed and efficiency improves. He wiggles his bottom, wobbles his head, and occasionally gets his whole body into the crawling act. His vocalizing indicates that he is enjoying this activity and turning it into a kind of play as well as a means of getting himself from one place to another. Babies especially like crawling all over beds, over and under the covers, pouncing on pillows and enjoying the freedom of movement and the soft, bouncy surfaces.

Scooting. A variation on crawling that serves as a prelude to standing is scooting. Watch your baby go from crawling to a kneeling position. He seems to wonder what to do next, which leads to scooting. Baby lifts one leg up while kneeling on and propelling himself forward with the other knee. Some babies scoot so well that they quickly lose interest in crawling.

Locomotion takes on a social aspect at this age. Crawling opens up a way for baby to approach you when he needs something or when he wants to play. Now he doesn't have to wait for you to come to him; he can come to you. To get your attention baby will crawl right up your pant leg, pulling himself up to a standing position, like a puppy eager to greet its owner.

Checking into home base. Notice that after baby crawls ten or fifteen feet away from you, he stops, turns, and looks back. He is checking to make sure that you are still there and is seeking your reassurance that it's okay to go further. This is a natural safety feature that accompanies normal separation anxiety.

Checking into home base

SCALING AND CLIMBING

When baby crawls up to the side of the bed or sofa he is faced with a challenge. He grabs the bedspread or upholstery and pulls himself up as far as he can go, a skill called scaling. This ability is a significant milestone. In scaling baby uses the reciprocal arm and leg movements he learned in cross crawling. To the master crawler, climbing and scaling are simply crawling upward rather than forward, a wonderful example of how one skill simply expands into another. Just as in the beginning of crawling, baby's arms work better than his legs in the learning stage. He first pulls up with both hands, while his legs are still partially bent and his feet curled inward. The next step is learning to use his arms in a hand-over-hand technique. Finally baby learns to push up with his legs while pulling with his hands.

Baby usually masters scaling up furniture rather quickly, but getting down is more difficult. Watch your baby after he scales up the side of his high chair and is standing, holding on with one hand. For a moment he appears stuck. When his wobbly

Scaling: crawling upward

legs give out, he may crumble quickly to the floor. Eventually he will learn to ease himself down in a style similar to the one he used to pull himself up. Letting himself down gently and carefully requires more skill than is required to pull himself up. You can teach your baby to ease his body down gently by supporting his hips and legs while he works himself down with his hands.

After baby masters scaling up tables, furniture, and crib rails, he will begin to explore climbing. Climbing steps is a favorite play activity at this age. Many babies can climb a whole flight of stairs by ten months, especially when encouraged by a cheering squad of proud parents and siblings.

Climbing stairs

Coming down is a more difficult feat to accomplish. Watch for the look of caution and the apprehension in his whole body as he approaches a stairway from the top. Baby will initially use his hands and arms as feelers to tell him when he is over the edge and how far it is to the next step down. Babies don't know intuitively that the safest way to get down stairs is backwards. They are likely to be confused at the top of a stairway and will either stop or come recklessly forward. Teach your baby to back down steps by turning his body around as he approaches the stairs. Show him how to dangle one foot over the edge of the step to touch the step below. Baby will then learn to use his feet to test the distance when climbing down steps or off a sofa. You will know that your baby can comfortably handle stairs when he swings his body around at the top of the stairway and approaches the second step foot first.

Safety awareness. Baby's desire to get around forges ahead of his capabilities. He can crawl and climb into dangerous situations that he is not yet ready to handle. Babies are fascinated by doors that open and gates that swing as they search for new challenges; a baby will naturally head for an open door or gate. If you put a safety gate at the top of the steps, it will tempt baby to crawl toward it and try to climb over or open it. It is wise not to rely solely on safety gates to protect baby from his natural curiosity. It is better to teach a baby how to back down stairs. However, if the stairs are uncarpeted or near an area where baby spends a lot of time, a safety gate is necessary.

Around ten or eleven months most babies will develop some caution about heights. They will stop and look and feel over the edge with their hands and feet as they approach a stairway or the edge of the bed. A watchful parental eye, however, is still important. More impulsive babies do not take the time to slow down and feel the edge and are likely to hurl themselves over onto the floor. The more impulsive your baby is, the more watchful and cautious you need to be. Babies whose crawling and climbing skills develop quickly are the ones who need the most monitoring.

STANDING

Standing supported

The skill of scaling leads to the next motor milestone, standing supported. In his first attempts at standing, baby supports himself with his arms and hands holding on to the side of a chair for dear life, while his legs and feet are trying to get it together. Notice that baby seems to stand with his feet uncomfortably rolled inward. When he learns to stand flat-footed with the toes turned out (almost like a ballerina), he can balance better.

You can tell the progress your baby is making at learning to stand by noticing the changes in how he scales up and leans against your leg. Initially, baby will pull up to a standing position by grabbing your pants and leaning most of his weight against your leg. Gradually you will feel less and less of his weight, and he will hold onto you more for balance than support.

Soon baby will begin stepping sideways while facing his support, holding on first with both hands, then with only one. After mastering this, baby turns sideways from his support, holds on with only one hand, and begins cruising along, placing one foot in front of the other. Baby will let go and stand all by himself momentarily until his legs give way and he "goes boom." As with learning to crawl, baby's upper body masters this skill before his legs do; his feet often cross and become entangled. When this happens watch the fascinating way baby compensates: he will turn his upper body to align with his lower half and thus stay balanced as he turns himself around to untangle his feet. Or he will simply fall down and start over.

As baby becomes more comfortable with standing his cruising abilities increase. He trips less during side-stepping and moves his hands and feet in a coordinated fashion. He wants to stand and play rather than sit. Put baby's toys on a low table, and he will entertain himself for five to ten minutes. Table-top play leads babies to explore objects on top of tables and desks. During the writing of this book my desk has been cleared off many times by the windshield-wiper arms of my young son, the desk-top explorer.

Besides cruising along next to furniture, baby also enjoys walking in front or along side of you, supported by your hands. This is a good way to help baby learn to place one foot in front of the other. If you cautiously let go first with one hand then the other, baby may momentarily stand on his own before crumpling down at your feet.

ON THE WAY TO WALKING

FROM SCALING AND CRUISING TO STANDING AND WALKING

The age at which babies walk unsupported varies greatly, from nine months to eighteen months. I have found that the average age of walking without support is twelve months. Rather impulsive infants tend to walk earlier but often walk less rhythmically and fall more often. More cautious infants tend to walk a little later, as if they are waiting until they are sure they can master the skill before attempting it. These more cautious infants tend to walk better when they do walk and are less accident-prone. The details of learning to walk vary greatly among babies, but most at least follow a similar sequence.

At first your baby cruises along, supporting himself with one hand, until one day he tries letting go. He teeters for a few moments and then collapses quickly, landing on his well-padded bottom. Once baby learns to plant his feet flat on the ground, turned out slightly, and to keep his knees from bending, he discovers that he can stand alone for a few more seconds. Next comes the balancing act. Baby opens his arms sideways and widens his stance in order to achieve better balance and stand for longer periods of time. You may notice that your baby's ankles roll inward when standing, exaggerating his flat-footed appearance. The ligaments that

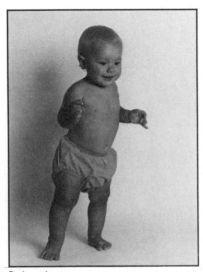

Balancing

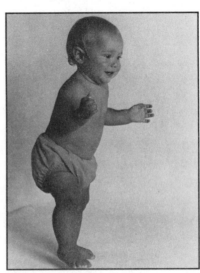

First steps

support the ankle are rubber-like at this age, and the arch of the foot is not yet well developed. Most babies appear flat-footed and weak-ankled until two or three years of age. Once baby learns to stand unsupported he is faced with two problems: how is he going to move forward and how is he going to get back down.

The motivation to begin walking or toddling often strikes when babies are cruising around and arrive at a gap between two pieces of furniture or between the furniture and a person. In order to continue and reach their goal, they will let go and toddle forward a few steps before falling. Baby's initial attempts at walking are quick and stiff-legged. He walks straight forward and looks like a waddling wooden soldier. On his face is an expression of wonder mixed with caution. His feet are only a few inches apart as he takes his early steps, and often they get tangled up in each other. As he learns to widen his stance and keep his legs six to eight inches apart his walking improves steadily. He can walk further and more rhythmically and begins to pivot, turning delightful circles as he practices his new skill. A toddler's walk bears little resemblance to an adult's. Walking is a balancing act for a beginner. There is no free, rhythmic arm-swinging; a toddler's arm and leg movements do not seem in harmony with each other because he is concentrating on using his arms to balance on one foot while he swings the other foot ahead.

The beginning walker falls frequently but you will notice that his falls gradually become more controlled. He will begin to fall by sitting down suddenly rather than falling forward. You will get the impression that his falls are more a result of lack of strength than lack of balance, though both factors are responsible.

As with any skill, parental reinforcement helps the baby's development. Take both your baby's hands and walk with him between your legs. Gradually let one hand go and then the other and allow him to stand by himself a moment before he tries to take a step. You can then hold him by one hand while he toddles at your side and you praise his efforts. It is amusing to watch beginning walkers toddle between two pieces of furniture. Their arms are held straight out, as if reaching for their final destination. Parents can reinforce their baby's attempts at walking by standing a few feet away from where baby is holding on and giving him an encouraging "Come on." Babies seem particularly motivated to take solo steps when they fix their eyes on a nearby object. The beginning walker seems to give some thought as to what mode of transportation to use. For example, I noticed that when I squatted a few feet away from our beginning walker, Matthew, he would want to come to me but did so by dropping to his knees and crawling. If he wanted to reach a nearby toy, he was more likely to take a few steps. I don't know what his reasons were for choosing one way over the other, but it seemed perfectly clear to him. Initially babies simply fall back down on their bottoms when they've had enough of standing, but eventually they learn to stoop down slowly into a crouch and gently lower themselves onto their knees and bottoms. Being able to squat down, pick something up, and stand again usually does not happen until after one year. It takes even longer for most babies to master the art of going from sitting to standing, with an intermediate stop at kneeling. Babies usually pass through a one- or two-month period of having to crawl over to something they can scale in order to get to a standing position. Sometime around the one-year mark, babies start going directly from the crawling to the standing position without using furniture (or a parent's legs) as a crutch. Kneeling is an early stage in achieving this free-standing position. Baby can get halfway to standing from a sitting position by balancing on one

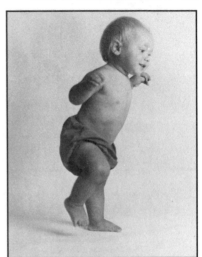

From crawl to squat to stand

or both knees and rocking forward and upward on his haunches. He often falls forward or backward as he tries to rise and balance on his feet. Baby begins to sense that crawling, scaling, and walking go together, each new skill being an extension of the previous one. He will quickly crawl toward his favorite piece of furniture, use it to pull himself into an upright position, and then toddle between pieces of furniture. Baby enjoys this mobility and often chuckles and sings to himself as he makes his rounds through the house.

The crawling-scaling-standing sequence opens up new play avenues for the curious explorer. Baby will crawl toward cabinets, open them, and pull out pots and pans. Babies are fascinated by cabinet doors and enjoy scaling up them and opening and closing them. They are also interested in large containers such as trash cans. You may observe your curious toddler scaling up the edge of a trash container, peering over the edge on tiptoes, and grabbing for anything in reach.

Shoes will help protect your baby's tender feet from rough surfaces, splinters, and sharp objects as he starts to get around on his own. The flat, even bottoms of a shoe provide stability in the balancing act of walking, and the insole provides a surface from which the baby's toes can push off. Shoes for your baby should have a bendable sole. The back of the shoe should be firm, and the top and sides flexible. Check your baby's shoes often (every six to eight weeks) to be sure he hasn't outgrown them.

Hand Skills and Hand Play

Around nine months baby develops a hand skill that is uniquely human—the ability to pick up objects between the thumb and forefinger. He puts his index finger directly on a tiny object and then curls the finger in as his thumb moves until the two meet and grasp the object, which, of course, is lifted to his mouth. He no longer needs to rest his whole arm on the table to support his hand while grasping objects. He lifts his whole arm to reach small pellets with his thumb and forefinger.

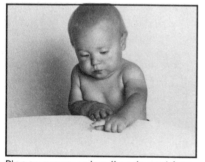

Pincer grasp: using thumb and forefinger to pick up a Cheerio.

Baby also uses his pointer finger to zero in on other objects such as the buttons on your shirt. Some mothers have reported to me that one of the first signs their babies show of being right- or left-handed is pointing. A baby may use his index finger as a pointer on the dominant hand before developing this ability in the non-dominant hand. Thumb and forefinger skills quickly lead to playing with blocks and containers.

BLOCK PLAY

Blocks may be the best toy ever invented. Watch what your baby does with a set of three or four hand-sized blocks. Baby picks up one block with one thumb and forefinger and another block in the other hand. He bangs the two together and bangs them on the table. He brings the two blocks together as if recognizing that they belong together. He will frequently be seen holding a block in each

Stacking—and toppling—a block tower

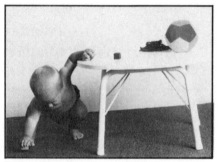

Baby holds his place while reaching down for a dropped block.

hand trying to match two sides together. This naturally leads to stacking. Around eleven or twelve months baby is often able to stack two blocks but usually can not release the top block smoothly enough to avoid toppling his little tower. He will often hold his place on the table with one hand while stooping over to pick up a dropped block with the other hand. This is a unique feature of play at this stage and coincides with the development of baby's memory.

Accommodation. By the last part of the first year, babies have learned to adjust their grasp to the size of the object while they are reaching for it. In this stage of development, baby begins to rotate his hand as he reaches, in order to pick up the object in the most efficient way. For example, if you place a pencil in front of your baby he will turn his hand parallel with the length of it before picking it up. The more varied are the objects available for baby to pick up, the more thought processes he must use in his play. Creating the opportunity for decision-making during hand play is an important way that parents can help baby's cognitive development.

Baby also learns to adjust for different weights of objects at this stage. When presented with an object that is heavier than expected, baby's hand and arm at first are pulled downward until he tenses his muscles and accommodates the unexpected weight. But the next time baby picks up the same object he adjusts his level of effort immediately so that his arm does not wobble or get pulled down. This is another example of how decision-making processes accompany hand play.

CONTAINER PLAY

Small objects definitely take priority over larger toys at this stage. Earlier, if you were to place a raisin next to a container, baby would have shown interest mainly in the larger container. Now, baby is likely to be more interested in the raisin than the container. Sometime around eleven to twelve months, he discovers the relationship between objects and containers. He investigates the emptiness of the container by putting his hand in it. He eventually grabs the raisin with one hand, the container with the other, and tries to insert the raisin into the container (if he doesn't eat it first). This is an extension of baby's developing hand skills. It is also a sign of his cognitive development. Baby must associate the block or toy in one hand with the openness of the container in the other. He has to realize that he can put the block into the container, but it takes him a while to learn to release the block. When he finally drops the block into the container he watches it fall with interest and enjoys hearing the sound it makes. He retrieves it with his fingers or dumps it out and starts the sequence again. He may even give the container a good shake before dumping out the object, adding a new dimension to the play pat-

Container play: drop the object in and shake it.

tern. Putting things in and taking them out of containers is one of the year-old baby's favorite activities.

Container play involves a lot of thinking. Baby must realize that the container and the block can come together. He has to determine how to bring them together. He must decide when to release the block and how to get the block back out again.

Around one year baby can begin to follow instructions in block and container play. When he plays with toy containers that have different shaped holes for matching blocks, you can show him, by pointing, which block fits through which hole, and he will usually follow your instructions and drop the right block though the right hole. Because baby has more interest in getting the block into the container rather than matching the shapes, he may want to remove the container's lid and put the blocks in directly. Baby may also follow your instructions when you show him how to stack blocks. However, his movements are still crude and likely to bring the whole tower tumbling to the floor. He does, however, have the idea of stacking blocks on top of one another. You will notice that during block play he gets a very serious look of concentration on his face; you know that he is thinking. Putting small objects in big containers becomes almost an obsession for baby, and a pile of small toys and large containers can send him into a frenzy of putting in and taking out. He becomes easily frustrated if an object doesn't fit.

Following instructions

A favorite game of older babies is opening and closing the cabinet doors, hauling out all the plastic containers and lids, and sitting on the floor in front of the cabinet trying to figure out what to do with all the pieces spread around them. Baby will try to fit the containers and the lids together, stack them inside each other, put them back in the cabinet, and bang them together or on the floor, talking and singing the whole time.

Self-feeding. The development of the thumb and forefinger pincer grasp makes it easier for baby to feed himself at this stage. Tasks initiated by the baby have greater learning value and usually hold his attention longer. Allowing baby to feed himself tiny morsels of soft food helps him pay attention during feedings. He is likely to spend more time putting his food in his mouth and will consume more food this way than if you tried to feed him with a spoon.

Safety Awareness

Babies' fascination for small objects and their ability to point, poke, and open require caretakers to be especially vigilant at this age. Caution older children (and yourselves) about leaving tiny mouthable objects in easy grasp of baby. Put safety latches on cabinet doors. Avoid letting enticing objects protrude over the edge of a counter, tempting baby to pull them down or climb up to get them. Periodically make safety tours around your house, looking for potentially dangerous situations from your baby's point of view. The best way of ensuring your child's safety is keeping one step ahead of him, anticipating problems before they occur.

Most babies have a built-in awareness of heights. A classic study, called the "Visual Cliff," was used to demonstrate that crawling infants can perceive a sudden change in distance from the ground. A checkerboard pattern was placed immediately under one half of the glass's surface. On the other half, the checkerboard was placed on the floor several feet beneath the glass. Babies were placed on the shallow side and encouraged to crawl toward the other side of the table, the deep side. The babies in the study were immediately aware of the apparent change in height and stopped crawling and peered over when they reached the cliff. However, particularly impulsive babies, called hurdlers, often do not respect their own sense of height and depth and are more likely to go over the edge.

Riding toys. Baby is now able to sit astride a riding toy and maintain his balance for a few feet of locomotion on wheels. Make sure the toy has a wide base of support and a low seat. Because baby's balance is still precarious on these little vehicles a parent should avoid letting baby ride on hard surfaces such as concrete. When baby wants to get off he just leans over and softly falls to the carpet or lawn.

Child-proofing. Because baby can now crawl, climb, and roll on wheels parents should be particularly vigilant in accident-proofing their home against the traveling explorer. Don't rely on safety gates. Gates and open doors seem to invite baby through, over, and out. Some babies are able to open sliding doors at this stage, so parents should be especially vigilant about keeping doors locked. Doors that open onto balconies are particularly inviting. Place chicken wire around the balcony railing to keep baby from slipping through if the rungs are spaced too far apart.

Shelves are favorites of babies at this stage. By placing toys on shelves approximately twelve to eighteen inches off the floor, baby can learn about taking things off and putting them back. He can select his toy and even use the shelving to help him stand and brace himself. This gives him a completely new perspective on playing. Sometimes baby will sweep his hand like a windshield wiper across the shelf, knocking off the toys. In our family we call this, "clearing the deck."

PLAYING OUTDOORS

As much as possible try to play with your child outdoors. Babies often seem more alert and fuss less outdoors, and attention spans seem longer. Movement, in general, attracts babies, and the rhythmical movement in nature—trees, water, clouds, animals, people—is especially interesting. Things are relatively stationary indoors.

Playing outdoors

Roll out the carpet. I enjoyed stacking games and container play with our eleven-month-old Matthew on a six-by-ten-foot piece of indoor/outdoor carpet on our patio. When we are not playing I keep the carpet inside rolled up next to a basket of toys. When I would say, "Matthew, let's go outside and play" and begin to roll out the carpet, he would anticipate the fun that would follow.

To your surprise, the kitchen may be baby's favorite play room, a place where he can use his new skills to "help" mom and dad. Because he can pull up and stand he can help unload the dishwasher. He gets especially excited if he can reach the silverware basket, so keep sharp knives out of his reach.

Cognitive Development

Many significant mental abilities appear in the last quarter of the first year. Memory plays a big part in these new skills. Being able to record and call up images is important to most learning skills and also to the gradual development of independence.

THE DEVELOPMENT OF MEMORY

In the last months of the first year, the infant greatly increases his ability to store and retrieve information. He develops the concept of **object** (and person) **permanence**. Previously things that were out of sight were out of mind. When a toy was hidden under a diaper, the infant made no effort to pursue it and quickly lost interest. But now the ability to make and retrieve mental images helps toys and people take on permanence. Even at this stage memory is still rudimentary, and baby often needs a cue to trigger the memory process. For example, when mother hears the baby fussing from another room, her calling out "Mama's coming" will help baby call up his mental image of her, and he may stop fussing, momentarily reassured that his mother is present, even if he can't see her.

THE SECURE BASE HYPOTHESIS

The ability to retain mental images of a familiar caregiver is thought to provide a secure base so the infant can move more easily from the familiar to the unfamiliar. The infant is now able to focus on one mental schema (mother comforting) while simultaneously engaging in another pattern of behavior (playing with a new toy). These new mental capabilities allow the infant to, in effect, take mother with him as he crawls further away from her to explore and learn from his environment. Cognitive development fosters motor development which in turn fosters more cognitive development. Another interesting feature of the secure base hypothesis is what I call the deep groove theory. Suppose the strength of mother-infant attachment is represented by the depth of the groove that records her image in baby's mental record. Early theories of infant behavior popularized the idea of spoiling which held that an infant who was strongly attached to his mother would never get out of this deep groove to become independent and explore his world. Experiments have shown the opposite to be true (Ainsworth 1972). The most securely attached infants, the ones with the deepest grooves, actually showed less anxiety when separating from their mothers to explore toys in the same room. They periodically checked in with mother (returning to the groove) for reassurance that it was okay to explore. The mother seems to add energy to the infant's explorations. Since the infant does not need to waste effort wor-

Mother's image, stored in his memory, helps baby feel secure when he is away from her.

rying about whether she is there, he can use that energy for exploration. An infant with a shallower attachment groove may not be able to avail himself of this energy conservation system.

This deep groove theory can also be used to explain why securely attached infants will not accept alternative ways of satisfying their needs. For example, some breastfed infants refuse to take a bottle. This is because a bottle does not fit into the anticipated pattern of behavior. When going from oneness to separateness, the securely attached baby establishes a balance between his desire to explore and encounter new situations and his continued need for the safety and contentment provided by mother. During each stage of development a baby strives to maintain an equilibrium between oneness and separateness. When a novel toy or a stranger upsets the balance and disturbs the baby beyond his level of coping or mother leaves and thus reduces his sense of security, the baby feels compelled to re-establish the original equilibrium. He calls out for his mother or he retreats from the strange situation. During a strange play situation a sort of "go ahead" message emanates from the mother that provides the infant with confidence to explore and handle the strange situation. If the infant moves closer to the mother or she comes to him, he picks up on this message and a new balance is established. The next time a similar situation is encountered the infant has confidence to handle it by himself without the mother. The consistent emotional availability of the mother promotes independence, confidence, and trust and culminates in the infant developing the capacity to be alone. One of the earliest theorists of mother-infant attachment (Bowlby 1969) suggests

> that a child with no confidence does not trust that his attachment figures will be accessible to him when he needs them. He adopts a clinging strategy to insure that they will be available. He is uncertain of the mother's availability and thus

is always preoccupied with it, this preoccupation hinders separation and exploration, and therefore his learning.

Secure attachment and later outcome. Studies have shown that infants who develop a secure attachment to mother during the first year are better able to tolerate separation from her when they are older (Cassidy 1984). Also, studies have shown that infants with difficult temperaments at risk for later behavioral problems are less likely to develop those problems if they are able to use mother as a secure base during the first year (Lewis 1985).

ASSOCIATIONS

The ability to associate two patterns of behavior to produce a novel reaction is one of the prime signs of cognitive development seen during the play activities at the end of the first year. For example, baby may begin using a stick to extend his reach. He may accidentally strike the stick against something else (or see another person do this), notice the sound which is produced, store this pattern in his memory, and reproduce it frequently. He notices that different effects are produced by different actions. The harder he bangs the drum, the louder the sound; different sticks and different drums produce different sounds. Container play and the matching of shapes are also play activities that are based on baby's developing cognitive ability to make associations.

Association: pie plates banged together go crash.

Play and Cognitive Development

Play and cognitive development are so interrelated that you cannot discuss one without talking about the other. Babies learn about their world through play, and parents and researchers can learn about what babies are thinking by watching them play. By observing and sharing in baby's play, parents can begin to get a faint idea of all the decision-making and problem-solving processes going on in baby's mind.

During baby's play you will notice that his learning is both a result of new developmental skills and the cause (or motivation) of his perfecting these skills and acquiring new skills through problem solving.

Baby's memory abilities seem to surge between nine and twelve months. He may be able to remember events that have occurred within the past twenty-four hours. One day we took our nine-month-old Matthew to the exhibit called "It's a Small World" at Disneyland. This exhibit includes a lot of music and visual stimulation which Matthew really enjoyed. The next day we sang the melody of the theme song to him, and his eyes and excited smile immediately showed us that he was remembering what he had seen and heard the day before. It is exciting to feel that you are able to shape your baby's thoughts by stimulating a recall of pleasing events.

Disappearing and reappearing games such as peek-a-boo and playing chase are favorites at this stage. Place a card in front of your face or a handkerchief

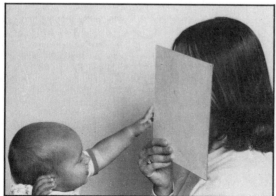 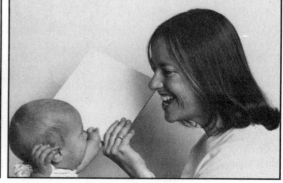

Peek-a-boo

over your head and maintain voice contact as you disappear, exclaiming, "Where's mommy?" As you suddenly reappear notice the delight on baby's face as he bursts into laughter. Sometimes baby may attempt to remove the obstacle himself, pulling the handkerchief from your face. Reverse peek-a-boo is also fun. Drape a diaper over baby's head, again maintaining voice contact ("Where's baby?"). As baby removes the covering and reappears exclaim, "There he is!" Peek-a-boo games stimulate baby's developing memory. It seems as if he stores the image of the disappearing parent momentarily in his memory, and when you reappear he takes delight in confirming that the image he sees is an accurate representation of the image he stored.

Associating pictures with real life. During this age baby begins to associate pictures in books with familiar objects in his environment. For example, when pointing at a picture of a cat while saying the word, baby may look around for the real cat. Baby is able to associate the word and the picture with his mental image of "cat." At ten months Matthew was afraid of dogs. When presented with a toy stuffed dog, he hesitated to play with it because it reminded him of the real thing. The ability to think of the real thing after being presented with an imitation is important to baby's growing imagination and memory.

Language Development

Between nine and twelve months baby makes great strides in verbal and body language. Your baby's receptive speech (his ability to understand) is several months ahead of expressive speech. For this reason, parents often underestimate how much a baby can understand, reasoning that because baby doesn't say much, he doesn't understand much. Babies comprehend much more than most people think.

RECEPTIVE LANGUAGE

The nine-to-twelve-month old will consistently respond to his name. He shows increasing interest during dinner conversations as if he catches the general drift of what's going on. He associates names with family members seated at the table and can correctly identify the right person when asked, "Where's Bob?"

Baby can usually understand simple, single directions, such as "Get the ball." Not until several months later can baby understand a sequence of directions such as "Get the ball and throw it to dad." For now, you must break things down into steps. First say "Get the ball." After baby has retrieved the ball add, "Throw the ball to daddy" and accompany this with appropriate throwing gestures. During this stage babies usually cannot follow simple directions without associated gestures. In the next stage of language development baby will be able to understand directions by hearing the words only.

As you become more aware that your baby understands what you say to him, you will naturally address him with more complex language, asking him simple questions that you know he understands and to which you can anticipate his responses: "Do you want to go for a walk?" or "Do you want to nurse?" Though baby is unlikely to reply with words you can usually tell what his answer is by the way his eyes, face, and body respond.

Sounds have meaning. At this age baby begins to recognize the words you say as symbols for objects in his environment. If you point to the sky and say "There's the moon" or "There's an airplane," your baby will eventually point to the moon or sky when you say the words.

The association of sounds with gestures and objects is an important milestone in your baby's language development. Notice how your baby makes these associations. Practice waving and saying "bye-bye" repeatedly, and then try using only the sound or the wave. Once baby has learned the sound-gesture association he may wave when hearing the sound or say something that sounds like "bye-bye" when he sees you wave.

Understanding "no." Between nine and twelve months most babies consistently respond to "no" and know that it means to stop whatever they are doing. How well baby understands and how quickly he responds depend a great deal on the gestures that accompany your "no." When baby is about to pull on a lamp cord, gently grab his exploring hand, look him in the eyes, and point to the cord while saying "No, don't touch—hurt baby!" Then redirect his curiosity to a safer and yet equally interesting activity. At this stage baby may even shake his own head "no" to mimic your gestures, as though this helps him understand.

Associating gestures with language: "So big!"

Besides showing greater understanding of language at this age, baby leaps forward in his expressive language—the words he says. His jabbering becomes more like talking. He produces long strings of continuous sounds with periodic, almost intelligible words entwined in his speeches. The inflections and changing intonations in his talking give you the feeling that baby thinks he is saying something even if you don't know what it is. Baby's sounds begin to acquire meaning to him and sometimes even to familiar listeners.

In language development, the term word means a sound used consistently to refer to an action or object, even if the sound is not intelligibly articulated. At this stage babies usually say familiar words ("Da-da," "Ma-ma," "cat") and familiar phrases ("night-night," "all done"). Babies like to imitate your sounds, including coughs and tongue noises such as clicks and hisses.

EXPRESSIVE LANGUAGE

MATURE CRYING

The nine- to twelve-month-old may stop crying when he anticipates that his need will soon be filled. Where before he might have continued crying until he was picked up, now he is able to turn off his crying when he sees you coming toward him. The ability to anticipate comfort reflects the pattern that has been set up in baby's memory since birth. He knows he can trust you to provide comfort after distress, so why keep on crying?

Your baby may develop more expressive crying, using more actual language with his cry to help you understand better why he is crying. There is less pitch in the cry and more form to the sounds so that the cry is indeed more expressive and language-like. Observers who are very sensitive to the quality of babies' cries tell me that they can tell a lot about a baby's attachment to his caregivers by the quality of his cry. Babies who have grown up in a responsive environment and who have learned to trust and anticipate caregivers' responses do not exhibit as much intensity and anger. Their cries are more quickly turned off because they've learned to anticipate a response. The baby who is a product of a less responsive environment expresses much more anger and panic, as if he does not expect a quick answer.

BODY LANGUAGE

Baby's body language improves greatly at this stage, especially the facial gesturing. Baby's expressive body language more easily tells you what he needs or wants. He pulls on your pants and raises his arms to get picked up. He squirms in your arms to tell you he needs a change of position or a new activity. Sometimes his need to get your attention is so intense that he may grab your nose and turn your face toward his. Baby becomes this expressive even before saying intelligible words.

Baby's body language is especially noticeable during feeding. He develops "nursing manners." He now squirms and twists himself into a comfortable fit into your lap. He may hook his legs over and under your arm to brace himself on your lap, fitting his body to yours during nursing. He may pull at your blouse to signal that he wants to nurse. When finished, he may push away and jabber something that resembles "all done." The combination of body language and sounds makes you feel that baby truly knows what he is saying.

Baby begins to use his tongue not only to make new and interesting sounds but also to gesture. For example, he may thrust out his tongue to push away a glass, indicating he does not want to drink. Baby enjoys listening to his own tongue and throat sounds. Sometimes he stops fussing to listen to his gargling sounds. Parenting seems a bit easier at this stage because your baby is much easier to read.

Waving "bye-bye." Up to this point, baby could imitate you waving good-bye. Now his language matures one step further; he may wave "bye-bye" without your prompting when leaving himself or watching others depart. Or, if you hold baby and wave "bye-bye," he may turn toward the door anticipating someone's departure. The ability to anticipate the events that follow these cue words is an important milestone in baby's language development.

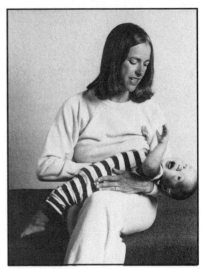

Nursing manners

Play should reinforce the major developmental milestones of a particular age. Appropriate play for the nine- to twelve-month-old should include locomotor activity, picking things up, and language skills. Babies love a game of pitch the ball and go fetch it. At this age babies can follow instructions such as, "Get the ball for daddy!" Use a small lightweight plastic ball. A ping-pong ball works well because it makes an interesting noise bouncing on the floor and it moves quickly; babies can grab hold of it and control it easily. Babies also like large balls that they can hold with two hands and throw to you from

LANGUAGE GAMES

"Get the ball."

over their heads. Babies love parents to sing to them while playing ball: "Roll the ball to daddy, baby roll the ball." Babies love to imitate and respond better to language that is accompanied by gestures such as in the games of pat-a-cake or peek-a-boo. Watch how your baby completes the pattern of action after you have given him the opening cue. For example, after playing many games of pat-a-cake, try saying pat-a-cake without moving your hands and you will often notice that baby will begin to clap his hands; you have touched off a pattern that has been stored in his memory. Be sure then, to reinforce baby's memory by joining in the game.

Keep games going. Baby reads your cues and responds, then you read his cues and respond, and the two of you continue the game. Harmony and mutual responsiveness take a while to develop, so don't be disturbed if your baby loses interest in your game. The average baby at this stage seems to have an attention span of less than one minute.

Language games reinforce learning correct words. For example, a parent says "bird" while pointing to a bird in the sky. Baby associates the sound with your gestures and with the bird he sees. When baby says what sounds like "bird" you acknowledge the correctness of this sound with a smile: "Yes, you've said bird!" Baby is then further motivated to repeat the word.

During language games parents will realize that language is becoming a cognitive skill. Notice that your baby sometime hesitates in order to determine whose turn it is to talk. It seems as if he is thinking about what you are saying and about his reply.

Under one year of age babies seem to be able to process only one word at a time, usually the last word in a sentence. It is fascinating how one simple word can trigger off a series of memories which in turn stimulate an action. For example, when I say, "Matthew, go!" the simple word "go" seems to call into Matthew's memory the idea of departure followed by images of a car ride, walking, playing outside, or any other activity associated with going out the door. In the next stage of development babies can comprehend more than a one-word memory message. When Matthew was one year of age and I said, "Matthew, go ocean!" he anticipated not only a departure through the door but also our usual walk to the ocean; if we turned in a direction that led away from the ocean he would protest. Language seems to condense packages of imagination and memory, allowing a simple word like "go" to open a whole package of outdoor activities and fun.

From nine to twelve months baby makes great strides in the ability to remember, think, and make decisions. You can see baby's emerging mental skills when you encourage him to seek out and find toys that are hidden from his view. In earlier stages of development, out of sight was out of mind, and baby quickly lost interest in a toy he couldn't easily find. Now baby shows interest in finding the hidden toy. Let baby see you place a favorite toy under one of two diapers lying in front of him. He will momentarily study the diapers as if trying to

LANGUAGE AND MEMORY DEVELOPMENT

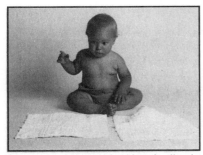

Remembering and looking for the toy

remember or figure out which diaper is covering the toy. Notice the decision-making expressions on his face. Once he makes his decision, he pulls off the diaper covering the toy and shows great delight in making the right choice. As baby gets older you can add to the complexity of this game and observe how your baby's cognitive development progresses. If you have consistently hidden the toy under the first diaper, even when baby sees you put the toy under the second diaper, most of the time he will initially search under the first diaper because that is what is in his memory. As his reasoning abilities develop, he will be able to realize that the toy is under the bulge in the second diaper or that if it isn't under the first diaper it must be hidden under the second.

The game of hide and seek also capitalizes on baby's developing language and memory skills. Chasing dad when he hides on his hands and knees behind the couch and peeks out saying "Here I am" encourages baby to use locomotor and memory skills. Baby will often imitate you by hiding and peeking around the couch himself. Try the game of sounding—playing chase with your voice around the house. Continue to call baby (by name, of course) from various rooms and watch him crawl or toddle around the house in search of you.

These little games are one more way of helping you to get to know your baby. Remember, that baby and parents develop *together*. During game play, try to imagine what your baby is thinking by the way he acts. The ability to get inside of your baby's mind is good training for handling discipline problems later on. Start now.

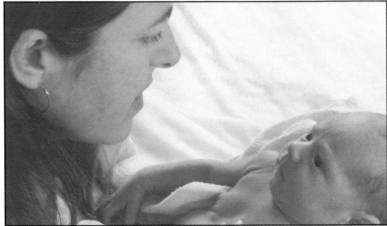

First meeting with mother

EARLY
SOCIAL
DEVELOPMENT

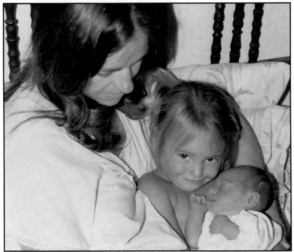

Siblings are an important part of baby's new family.

Mother can be trusted to bring comfort—an important early lesson.

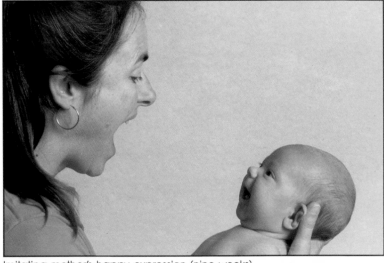

Imitating mother's happy expression (nine weeks)

INITIATING
SOCIAL INTERACTION

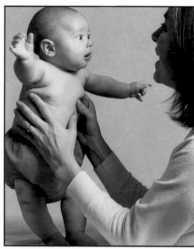

Dialoguing with mother (four months)

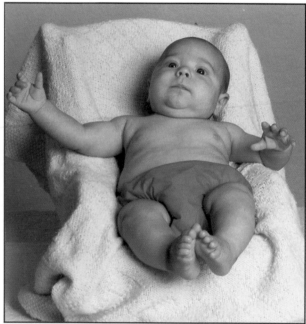

Open hands, open eyes mean baby is ready to play
(three months)

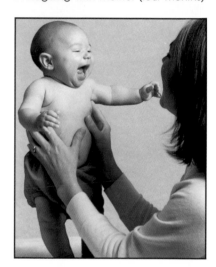

Reaching out to start a conversation (five months)

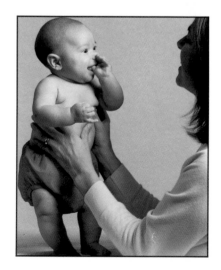

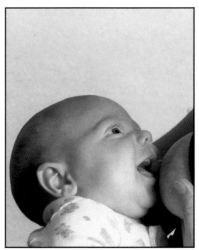

A nursing conversation (three months)

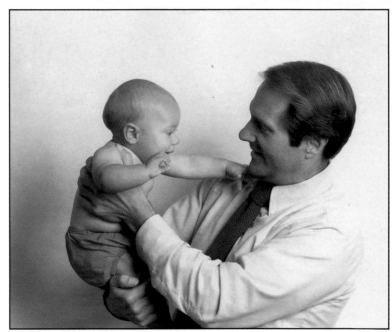

Social directing: "Let's play!"

Nursing manners (six months)

Touching and grooming mother (six months)

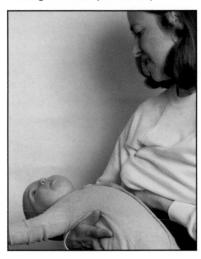

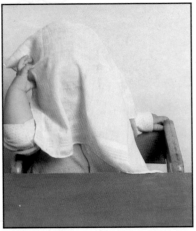 

Peek-a-boo!

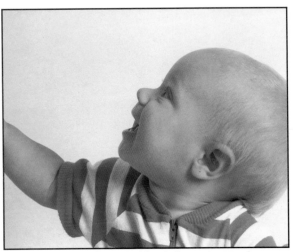 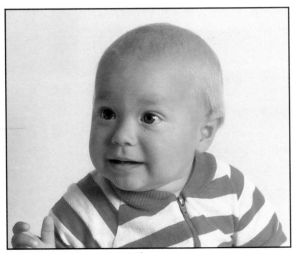

Baby's expressive face and body language make communication easier (nine months).

Happy Birthday

SUMMARY: *NINE TO TWELVE MONTHS*

• Masters cross-crawling; may also scoot across floor.

• Scales and climbs furniture.

• Squats to pick up toy while holding onto furniture with one hand.

• Crawls up stairs; coming down is harder.

• First steps alone: stiff-legged, falls frequently. Experiments with various steps; pivots.

• Pushes up from bear crawl to squat to stand and walk.

Large motor

• Pincer grasp well-developed; points and pokes with index finger; uses index finger and thumb to pick up tiny objects.

• Turns hand to accommodate shape, dimensions of objects.

• Can stack blocks; holds place with one hand when retrieving dropped block. Drops blocks in container, dumps them out.

• Hand dominance becomes apparent.

• Uses hands to shield eyes from sun, pour water from cup, clear off desk tops, pull on mother's blouse to nurse.

Fine motor

• Both receptive and expressive language improve.

• Uses simple words: mama, dada, ball, cat, go. Understands labels, "no."

• Babbles short sentences.

• Understands simple directions when accompanied by gestures.

• Understands and imitates simple phrases and gestures: "bye-bye," "night-night," "all done."

Language/ social

• Pulls up on pant legs, signalling "pick me up."

• Develops awareness of heights; stops at top of stairs.

• Follows your voice around the house.

• "Helps" mommy in kitchen.

• Stronger protests when expectations not met.

• Separation and stranger anxieties continue.

• Memory develops; object permanance begins. Shows memory of recent events.

• Associates pictures in books with real events.

Cognitive/ play

Ainsworth, M. D. S. and Bell, S. M. 1974. Mother-infant interaction and the development of competence. In *Growth of Competence*, eds. K. Connolly and J. Bruner, New York: Academic Press.

Ainsworth, M. D. S. 1978. *Patterns of attachment*. Hillsdale, New Jersey: Lawrence Erlbaum Company.

Ainsworth, M. 1979. Attachment: retrospect and prospect. Paper presented to Society for Research in Child Development, San Francisco, March 1979.

Anderson, G. C. 1977. The mother and her newborn: mutual caregivers. *JOGN Nurs* September, pp. 50-57.

Anthony, E. J. 1984. The influence babies bring to their offspring. In *Frontiers of Infant Psychiatry*, vol. 2, eds. J. Call et al. New York: Basic Books, 1984.

Beckwith, L. 1971. Relationship between attributes of mothers and their infants' I. Q. scores. *Child Dev* 42:1083-97.

Bell, S. M. 1970. The development of the concept of object as related to infant-mother attachment. *Child Dev* 41:291-311.

Bell, S. M. and Ainsworth, M. D. S. 1972. Infant crying and maternal responsiveness. *Child Dev* 43:1171.

Bower, T. G. R. 1982. *Development in Infancy*. San Francisco: W. H. Freeman.

Bowlby, J. 1969. *Attachment and Loss*. New York: Basic Books.

Broad, F. 1972. Effect of breastfeeding on later speech development. *New Zealand J Med* 482:28-31.

Butler, S. R. et al. 1978. Maternal behavior as a regulator of polyamine biosynthesis in brain and heart of developing rat pups. *Science* 199:445-47.

Carpenter, G. 1980. Epidermal growth factor is a major growth-promoting agent in human milk. *Science* 210:198-99.

Case, R. 1985. *Intellectual Development, Birth to Adulthood*. New York: Academic Press.

Cassidy, J. and Main, M. 1984. The relationship between infant-parent attachment and the ability to tolerate brief separation at six years. In *Frontiers of Infant Psychiatry*, vol. 2, eds. J. Call et al. New York: Basic Books.

Condon, W. S. and Sander, L. 1974. Neonate movement is synchronized with adult speech. *Science* 183:94-101.

Diamond, M. A. 1984. Cortical change in response to environmental enrichment and impoverishment. In *The Many Facets of Touch*. Johnson and Johnson Roundtable No. 10, pp. 22-29.

Douglas, J. W. B. 1950. Extent of breastfeeding in Great Britain in 1946 with special reference to health and survival of children. *J Obstet Gynaecol* 57:355.

Emde, R. N. and Harrison, R. J. *The Development of Attachment and Affiliative Systems*. New York: Plenum Press.

Erikson, E. H. 1968. *Identity, Youth and Crisis.* New York: Norton.

Geber, M. 1958. The psycho-motor development of African children in the first year and the influence of maternal behavior. *J Soc Psychol* 47:185.

Graf, M. V. et al. 1984. Presence of delta-sleep-inducing peptide-like material in human milk. *J Clin Endocrinol Metab* 59:127.

Hoeffer, C. and Hardy, M. C. 1929. Later development of breast fed and artifically fed infants *J Am Med Assoc* 92:615.

Hofer, M. 1982. Some thoughts on the transduction of experience from a developmental perspective. *Psychosom Med* 44:19.

Hofer, M. 1978. Parental contributions to the development of their offspring. In *Perspectives in Ethology,* eds. P. Bateson and P. Klopfer. New York: Plenum Press.

Hunziker, U. A. and Barr, R. G. 1986. Increased carrying reduces infant crying: a randomized controlled trial. *Pediatrics* 77:641-48.

Kagan, J. 1984. *The Nature of the Child.* New York: Basic Books.

Korner, A. F. and Thoman, E. B. 1970. Visual alertness in neonates as evoked by maternal care. *J Exp Child Psychol* 10:67-78.

Kuhn, C. M. et al. 1978. Selective depression of serum growth hormone during maternal deprivation in rat pups. *Science* 201:1035-36.

Lawrence, R. A. 1980. *Breastfeeding: A Guide for the Medical Profession.* St. Louis: C. V. Mosby.

Lewis, M. 1985. Effect of caregiver responsiveness on infant development. Keynote address, American Academy of Pediatrics, San Antonio, October 1985.

Lozoff, B. 1979. Infant care: Cache or carry. *J Pediatr* 95:478-83.

MacFarlane, A. 1975. Olfaction in the development of social preference in the human neonate. CIBA Foundation Symposium No. 33. New York: Associated Scientific Publishers, Inc.

Meltzoff, A. N. and Moore, M. K. 1977. Imitation of facial gestures by human neonates. *Science* 198:75-78.

Montaque, A. 1971. *Touching: The Human Significance of the Skin.* New York: Columbia University Press.

Papousek, H. 1984. The evolution of parent-infant attachment; new psychobiological perspective. In *Frontiers in Infant Psychiatry,* eds. J. Call, et al. New York: Basic Books.

Piaget, J. 1952. *The Origins of Intelligence in Children.* New York: Norton.

Prechtl, H. F. R. and O'Brien, M. J. 1982. Behavioral states of the full term newborn. In *Psychology of the Human Newborn.* New York: John Wiley.

Sander, L. W. et al. 1970. Early mother-infant interaction and 24-hour patterns of activity and sleep. *J Child Psych* 9:103-23.

Sears, W. 1982. *Creative Parenting*. New York: Dodd Mead.

Tennes, K. 1982. The roles of hormones in mother-infant transactions. In *The Development of Attachment and Affiliative Systems*, eds. P. Buteson and P. Klopfer. New York: Plenum Press.